PHANTOMS:
Experiences and Investigations

ALSO BY D. SCOTT ROGO

Nad: A Study of Some Unusual Other-World Experiences
A Psychic Study of "The Music of the Spheres"
Methods and Models for Education in Parapsychology
The Welcoming Silence

PHANTOMS:
Experiences and Investigations

D. Scott Rogo

DAVID & CHARLES
NEWTON ABBOT LONDON VANCOUVER

ISBN 0 7153 6824 9

First published in Great Britain in 1976 by
David & Charles (Publishers) Limited

Printed in Great Britain
by Redwood Burn Ltd Trowbridge and Esher
for David & Charles (Publishers) Limited
Brunel House Newton Abbot Devon

Published in Canada
by Douglas David & Charles Limited
1875 Welch Street North Vancouver BC

To

Gary R. Lynn

and

Ernie Harris

PUBLISHER'S NOTE

For greater readability, numbered references have been omitted from the text. Notes and references by chapter, at the back of the book, give the sources of information for those who may wish to pursue these topics further.

contents

illustrations

preface

Psychical research is the science which deals with the study of such topics as extrasensory perception, mind over matter, precognition, apparitions and hauntings, and various other paranormal phenomena. The history of psychical research as a science dates back to Victorian England, when a group of Cambridge scholars felt that beyond a morass of charlatanry, self-delusion, and errors of observation, there might well be a speck of truth in the tales of ESP and apparitions which had been recorded throughout man's history. Slowly but surely these men, who founded the Society for Psychical Research in 1882, amassed hundreds of well-documented cases of apparitions, hauntings, and other extrasensory encounters.

Psychical research, or parapsychology, can be approached from two different angles. First there is the experimental approach. This approach was made famous by Dr. J. B. Rhine, who pioneered scientific recognition of ESP in his experiments at Duke University in the 1930s. In these experiments a subject would try to guess, by ESP, which of five geometric symbols (star, cross, wavy lines, circle, or square) were impressed on cards concentrated upon by the experimenter. As is well known, many subjects tested were able to call the correct symbol astronomically above what pure chance would have allowed. The experimental approach is not a new one in parapsychology. Years earlier a French physiologist and Nobel prize-winner, Charles Richet, conducted experiments in which his subjects were asked to guess the suit of playing cards. Some of his subjects were amazingly successful.

Parapsychology today has elaborated on these procedures, but most ESP experiments rely heavily on statistics to determine if the subject's results were beyond what the laws of chance would allow, very similar to the way Rhine assessed his early experiments.

Despite the fact that psychical research is today an experimental science, its basis still remains in the testimony of millions of people who have had their own personal psychic experiences. The study of these spontaneous cases is a second approach to parapsychology. The way that psychical events manifest in our day-to-day living can offer insights into the process of psychical phenomena that may well elude us in the laboratory. Further, no amount of laboratory findings can ever bring the same inner conviction that the mind has no physical boundaries as that which one experiences himself.

An apparition is a type of psychical phenomenon that cannot be isolated in the laboratory. It cannot be placed under the biologist's microscope or dissected on the surgeon's table. To understand apparitions and hauntings we must delve into the chronicles of those who have had firsthand experiences with them. Placed side by side with the experiments carried out in parapsychological laboratories, human narrative and testimony is also a key to our understanding of the unexplored mysteries of human existence and the transcending abilities of the human mind.

For hundreds of years, secreted in diaries and letters, camouflaged in novels and stories, and confided to friends and relatives, people have chronicled their meetings with phantom visitors. It took the labor of many dedicated scientists to gradually evaluate these experiences.

In this book I hope to illustrate the many different kinds of encounters people have had with phantoms, hauntings, and other psychical events. It is now time that parapsychology turn back to the study of these half-forgotten narratives in order to further penetrate man and nature's innermost secrets.

D. Scott Rogo

ONE

a variety of phantoms

Phantoms, apparitions, wraiths, ghosts, specters—it is remarkable how our language has evolved so many words for creatures which most people do not even believe exist. Yet, although ghostly visitants and omen-bearing wraiths have usually been relegated to storybooks and campfire tales, over countless centuries hundreds of people have chronicled their encounters with them. These are the people this book will be concerned with. Those who have had some encounter with phantoms and those scientists who have tried to fathom their mystery.

There are many types of apparitional experiences, and apparitions tend to group into certain classifications. G. N. M. Tyrrell, a former president of the Society for Psychical Research (SPR), spent considerable time classifying apparitions, theorizing about them, and writing about them. Tyrrell grouped apparitions into four main categories and these classifications are generally accepted as representing the major types of apparitions that have been recorded.

First are the experimental apparitions. These are the result of one person consciously trying to project an image of himself to another individual.

Second are the crisis apparitions. These are recognized phantom forms of friends or relatives which appear at the same time that the person is undergoing some great crisis, accident, injury, or death.

Third are the post-mortem apparitions (apparitions of the dead) seen long after the person represented by the apparition has died.

Fourth are the continual apparitions, or ghosts, to use a common term. These catagories denote the main types of phantoms, and so let us begin this adventure into the unknown by exploring them.

There is adequate evidence to prove that one mind can pick up the thoughts of another mind and can even visualize the data through ESP.* A pioneer who demonstrated this was Upton Sinclair, who besides his writings and social commentary was an avid student of psychical research. His investigations in this field have given parapsychology some valuable records. In the research he carried out, his wife would try to visualize certain simple pictures which her husband or others concentrated on. Sometimes these experiments were carried out from room to room, other times from up to forty miles away. All told, of two hundred and ninety experiments, 23 percent were successful, 53 percent partially so, and 24 percent were failures. If one can envision telepathically based or clairvoyant pictures, it seems plausible that one might also send a picture of himself over distances to be received and projected as an apparition.

One man who succeeded in this was a friend of William James, the pioneering American philosopher-psychologist. James's friend, a Harvard professor whose identity James kept confidential, one night attempted to project himself to a lady friend. The professor

* Few would doubt that a mass of evidence is available showing an ability of the mind to obtain knowledge it could not have come by normally. One could cite a great accumulation of scientific evidence for ESP. In 1920 at Groningen University in Holland, an epoch-making experiment was carried out by three professors: Drs. Heymans, Brugmans, and Wynberg. The experimental subject was a youth named van Dam. This experiment was foolproof. Van Dam, blindfolded, was seated before a checkerboardlike panel, divided into forty-eight squares, six by eight columns. The columns were marked A to H, 1 to 6. In the room directly above were the experimenters with a small opening in the floor so that they could watch their subject. These scientists proceeded to select randomly two cards—one a number, one a letter—which would indicate one square on the board in front of van Dam, for him to guess. One hundred and eighty-seven trials were made. By the rules of chance, van Dam should have accurately "guessed" four correct squares. Yet, by some uncanny and not understood faculty he correctly pointed to sixty squares concentrated upon by the eager and baffled experimenters. Certainly the odds are so beyond chance that no theory of "coincidence" could possibly explain it.

reported the incident to James, who in turn sent it to the American Society for Psychical Research (ASPR). The professor began the experiment at about 9:45 P.M., but after only ten minutes gave it up. However, the next day the woman excitedly told him that while at supper she thought she had seen his figure peering through the crack of the dining room door. She noted that it was 10:00 P.M. Upon investigating she could not find him anywhere in the house.

One of the best-documented experimental apparitions is that of S. H. Beard, an enterprising young man who attempted to project his apparition to his fiancée Miss L. S. Verity. His first experiment was an attempt to appear in his fiancée's bedroom, which she shared with her eleven-year-old sister. Although Miss Verity did not know of the experiment she suddenly saw the recognizable figure of her betrothed. In true Victorian melodramatic tradition, she screamed, waking her sister, who also saw the phantom. Beard was a friend of Edmund Gurney and kept him abreast of his experiences and also the corroborative statements supplied by his fiancée. Gurney placed these experiments in his co-authored and carefully documented compilation *Phantasms of the Living*.

What are we to make of this experience? Some will say that Beard projected his double, an ultraphysical apparitional body, to the girls. Others will see it as a unique experiment in telepathy, where the receiver unconsciously projected this impulse into a telepathic hallucination, similar to the mental pictures Mrs. Sinclair was able to consciously visualize.

Crisis apparitions are the next point of inquiry. There is considerable evidence that emotional and physical traumas will prompt psychic experiences. Experiences in the face of threat are not restricted to apparitions. Telepathic experiences of all sorts have been recorded. Recently, Ian Stevenson, a psychiatrist who has devoted many years to parapsychology and who heads a division of parapsychology at the University of Virginia School of Medicine, has presented thirty-five cases wherein someone has become aware of a vague impression of crisis. The following case of Mrs. Joicey Asher Hurth is typical.

Mrs. Hurth's five-year-old daughter, Joicey, came home from a birthday party to find to her dismay that her father and brother had already left for the local movie theater. Prompted by her mother, Joicey went to meet them. Mrs. Hurth had returned to her kitchen chores when, ''Quite suddenly while I held a plate in my hand an awesome feeling came over me. I dropped the plate, turned my eyes toward heaven, and prayed aloud, 'Oh, God, don't let her get killed.' '' Mrs. Hurth at that moment became aware that her daughter had been hit by a car. Anxiously, she called the theater only to be told by a somewhat startled ticket taker that her daughter had just been hit by a car. Luckily the girl was only stunned. By one of those mysterious dynamics of human communication Joicey's cry of ''Mama, Mama, I want my Mama'' had been picked up by a mental process we are only beginning to understand.

Mrs. Hurth's experience, while dramatic, is not unique. Hundreds of people have had the same extrasensory encounter, for the crisis situation is a rich breeding ground of the appearances of apparitions. The following is a well-documented case.

Eldred Bowyer-Bower was one of the hundreds of men who died during the terrible years of World War I. On March 19, 1917, his plane was shot down over France. Hundreds of miles away in India his half sister, engaged in caring for her baby, had this experience: ''My brother appeared to me on the 19th March, 1917. At the time I was either sewing or talking to my baby—I cannot remember quite what I was doing at that moment. The baby was on the bed. I had a very strong feeling that I must turn round; on doing so I saw my brother, Eldred W. Bowyer-Bower. Thinking he was alive and had been sent out to India, I was simply delighted to see him and turned round quickly to put baby in a safe place on the bed, so that I could go on talking to my brother; then turned again and put my hand out to him, when I found he was not there. I thought he was only joking so I called him and looked everywhere I could think of looking. It was only when I could not find him I became very frightened and had the awful fear that he might be dead. . . .''

Mrs. Paquet was another unwitting traveler across some uncanny frontier. Mrs. Paquet awoke one morning feeling depressed and mildly upset. Hoping that a stiff cup of tea might banish her gloom, she suddenly found herself faced with a spectral sight: ''. . . as I turned around my brother Edmund—or his exact image—stood before me and only a few feet away. The apparition stood with back toward me, or rather, partially so, and was in the act of falling forward—away from me—seemingly impelled by two loops or a loop of rope drawing against his legs. The vision lasted but a moment, disappearing over a low railing or bulwark, but was very distinct. I dropped the tea, clasped my hands to my face, and exclaimed, "My God! Ed is drowned?"

Indeed this tragedy had taken place six hours previously. The apparition was so vivid that Mrs. Paquet had even noticed his rolled-up pant legs revealing a white lining. This was later verified.

One problem with quoting narratives such as these is, naturally, how much stock can be placed on human testimony? Where human testimony is concerned, proof will never be forthcoming. As with any religious or cosmic experience, such preternatural events, while giving complete conviction to the percipient, cannot bring that same conviction to others. Even if the experience is corroborated by outside witnesses, such as the theater ticket taker who answered Mrs. Hurth's anguished phone call, evidence is strong but one cannot think in terms of actual proof. But, when hundreds of individuals have reported apparitions, sometimes collectively (that is, seen by more than one person at the same time), this evidence arranges itself into an unbreakable bundle of sticks which cannot be fractured by all the doubting that the "rational" mind can elicit.

Unfortunately, apparitions, unlike many psychic phenomena such as ESP, cannot be so easily captured by study in the laboratory. While ESP has been saved from the rather problem-ridden and subjective nature of human testimony by the use of statistical tests, apparitions still seem to be prompted by emotional and psychological conditions so intricate that so far no one dares to believe that this phenomenon can be isolated, even if elusively, in an experimental setting. Thus, belief in apparitions must still remain within the province of the scientifically unfashionable.

Yet, one could argue, if telepathy can affect our dreams and our biological functions, could it not affect our senses too? Few would deny this. An apparition might be defined as some sort of extrasensory effect on our sense of sight. In this light apparitions are perfectly believable in the consideration of the evidence for telepathy. Thus, ESP and apparitional cases are mutually concordant.

Whether or not apparitions may ultimately be shown to result from such an extrasensory effect akin to telepathy is a moot point in parapsychological circles. Yet, most likely, the two do share a similar mechanism.

But, apparitions have gone beyond the realm of crisis experiences or the willful projections of some experimenters. For apparitions have appeared that represent those who have been dead for many years.

From time immemorial there have been tales of the dead returning to the living. Psychical research for many years was devoted to the search for evidence that man's personality, so little understood by the infant study of psychology at the close of the Victorian age, could survive the death of the body. At that time the recent writings of Darwin had undermined the religious tenets that had cohesively bound European and American culture. People were looking for new gods to worship and scientific methodology, with John Stuart Mill at its head, offered a bold new altar on which to rest one's faith. In line with this new materialism some philosophers felt that psychical manifestations might once again preserve the religious beliefs and values that had been a cultural mainstay. The doctrine of immortality was one of the hardest hit of Christian dogmas, and in their search for evidence of immortality the early psychical researchers were drawn into the study of Spiritualism, at the time a new American religion that had just reached England a few years before. The Spiritualists claimed that the dead still influenced the living and that through mediums they could speak to us and as apparitions they could appear to us.

Frederic Myers, one of the founders of the Society for Psychical Research, was deeply involved in the study of apparitions of the dead and collected many such accounts. These were not the testimonies of spiritualists or religious zealots, but of everyday men and women who walked London's pedestrian streets.

The following incident is not dramatic. As in most authentic ghost stories there is no atmosphere of foreboding, climax, or denouement. Instead, it is a startling, though plain, experience.

Mrs. Mabel Booth recounted the experience to Myers, who collected the additional verification.

On the 10th of April, 1889, at about half-past nine o'clock A.M.

> my youngest brother and I were going down a flight of stairs leading to the kitchen to fetch food for my chickens, as usual. We were about half way down, my brother a few steps in advance of me, when he suddenly said—"Why, there's John Blaney, I didn't know he was in the house!" John Blaney was a boy who lived not far from us, and he had been employed in the house as hall-boy not long before. I said that I was sure it was not he (for I knew he had left some months previously on account of ill-health), and looked down into the passage but saw no one. The passage was a long one, with rather a sharp turn in it, so we ran quickly down the last few steps and looked round the corner, but nobody was there, and the only door he could have gone through was shut. As we went upstairs my brother said, "How pale and ill John looked, and why did he stare so?" I asked what he was doing. My brother answered that he had his sleeves turned up, and was wearing a large green apron, such as the footmen always wear at their work. An hour or two afterwards I asked my maid how long John Blaney had been back in the house? She seemed much surprised and said, "Didn't you hear, Miss, that he died this morning?" On inquiry we found he had died about two hours before my brother saw him. . . .

Myers was able to get a statement from the percipient himself; "We were going downstairs to get food for Mabel's fowl, when I saw John Blaney walking round the corner. I said to Mabel, 'That's John Blaney!' but she could not see him. When we came up afterwards we found he was dead. He seemed to me to look rather ill. He looked yellow, his eyes looked hollow and he had a green apron on."

Apparitions of the dead have also been seen many years after physical death. The following has become a classic in psychical research literature.

At the youthful age of eighteen, F. G.'s sister died of cholera.* Nine years later F. G. had all but forgotten his sister during his day-to-day existence as a commercial traveler which had brought him to St. Joseph, Missouri. In his room at the Pacific House, that noon, while busily filling out his orders and smoking, he became aware of another presence in the room standing by his side. Turning toward it, he was confronted by the apparition of his deceased

* In the early years of psychical research the anonymity of those reporting psychic experiences was often maintained. However, the correct names were always filed in the original report with the journal in which the account would appear.

sister, disfigured by a long red scratch on her right cheek. When F. G. reported his experience to his parents, his mother was overcome with emotion and admitted that while caring for the body before burial she had accidentally scratched the girl's lifeless face and had covered up the scratch with make-up. She had told no one of the incident.

The case was investigated by Richard Hodgson, one of the first pioneering psychical investigators in the United States. Though a fervent exposer of psychic fakery and sham, Hodgson was most impressed by the case.

One argument often used to denigrate the evidence for the existence of apparitions is that while these experiences seem to have occurred many years ago, they don't seem to happen today. It is true that more apparitional cases were published during parapsychology's infancy. The reason for this is understandable for at that time parapsychology had not yet evolved from anecdote to experiment and the early researchers were much more interested in collecting cases than they are now. So few cases find their way into psychic literature today and they are lost in the huge body of experimental studies which have engulfed the field.

Andrew MacKenzie is one of the few writers interested in psychical research who has attempted to collect modern cases of apparitions. Combining a sophisticated attitude toward psychical research with a flair for journalism, MacKenzie has published several new cases of apparitions.

To show that even in our mechanized society, where we pride ourselves on our scientific technology and advanced intellect, the shadowy forms of the dead still hover about us, only one example need be quoted: ''During the war I had a bed in an indoor shelter in my hall,'' Mrs. Gill wrote to Mr. MacKenzie, ''and in September 1943 I was resting about midnight and awaiting my call for 1 A.M. duty in the wardens' post outside my drive gates, when a woman in a morning dress of Victorian age 'floated' through the closed door of my music room, which faced me, and went through the closed front door. Ten days later a friend who had heard my story produced a head-and-shoulders photograph of the woman I had seen. She was a Mrs. Drake who had been mistress of my house more than seventy years before. . . .''

Mrs. Gill had never seen the photograph before or heard of Mrs. Drake prior to her unearthly encounter.

If some phantoms are startling, others can best be described as persistent. One of the most tenacious wraiths ever recorded was that of Palladia, a young girl who died at the age of fifteen. Over many years her form appeared to Eugene Mamtchitch, a Russian official. The story is a sad one. Eugene and Palladia had met in 1870. Palladia was put into a convent and Eugene and her brother tried to secure her release. Finally, two years later they were successful. After leaving the convent Eugene traveled with the girl to Crimea, a town by the Black Sea, and left to return to Kiev. A year later, after the two had met only once more, Palladia died.

Long after, at a séance, messages from Palladia were directed to Eugene via a table that rapped out messages to him (raps are percussive sounds that often indicate the letters of the alphabet). On returning home Eugene got raps at his own table.

In October 1876 the drama began. While playing a new piano in his comfortable apartment in Kiev, Eugene saw a phantasm in the doorway that he recognized as Palladia. Eugene could only stop playing and stare of the fantastic figure. The apparition began to move and he rushed forward toward it. He stopped as his friend, Potolof, appeared from another room, puzzled as to why the playing had stopped so abruptly.

Three years later, while Eugene was at his desk writing, the same other-world guest appeared, seated in an armchair. He tried to talk to her, asking how she felt. He heard a voice utter a quiet one-word reply. While he watched the figure it gradually faded away. On another occasion the figure appeared while Eugene's dog was with him. The setter growled, its hair on end, and then in a fit of inexplicable terror tried to hide. The same morning Sophie, Eugene's sister, had felt an unseen presence and heard a disembodied voice speak to her. Some years later, Eugene's little son also saw the figure.

The apparition of Palladia is what, in common parlance, one would call a ghost. Phantoms of the living, dying, and dead are usually fleeting once-in-a-lifetime experiences. Yet, on rare occasions these forms may be trapped by some delicate condition that gives rise to psychic phenomena. From then on they might be seen over several years by different viewers.

There are many theories of what ghosts are. Some hold the traditional view that they are personalities who have not been able to make the complete transition into death. Others link ghosts to ESP and, in particular, psychometry. Psychometry is a type of clairvoyance where the subject receives extrasensory information by placing himself in physical contact with an object. Throughout the history of psychical research there have been many gifted subjects with this uncanny ability. In France, Gustave Geley, a physiologist, investigated the abilities of a Polish engineer, Stephan Ossowiecki, and found that if he were even to touch an object he would often become flooded by impressions about it or its handlers.

In Mexico, a German doctor, G. Pagenstecher, discovered the same ability with one of his subjects, Señora Maria Reyes de Zierold. Once, given a piece of pumice, she vividly reenacted the great tragedy of Pompeii. The stone, taken from the Pompeii ruins, was handed to her while she was hypnotized. On another occasion she was given an identification string of a soldier. Immediately the girl became agitated as visions of a battlefield loomed before her tightly closed eyes. She saw three men standing behind a fourth. An exploding bomb disrupted the scene, death was present, and moaning was heard by the psychic. In fact, a perfect description was given of the scene leading to the death of the soldier whose identification string she held.

In these cases, gifted people have been able somehow to contact a memory bank by coming into touch with a physical object. Some psychical researchers have felt that in some instances the traces can be so viewed that anyone might perceive them. A haunted house is such an environment where one ''psychometrizes'' an entire house, seeing a replay of scenes and sounds as though a cosmic television set had been switched on. Mrs. Eleanor Sidgwick, one of the able women of parapsychology's past, promoted this theory, as did Professor H. H. Price, a philosopher whose thoughts had been formed in part through a close association with psychical studies.

No matter what one wishes to believe about hauntings, they do represent another form of apparitional experience, as Rose Despard discovered and repeatedly observed from 1882 to 1889.

"A Record of a Haunted House" was the title under which Rose Despard (named Morton in the report) published her observations of the ghost that walked the home in which she lived in Cheltenham, England. Far from a fanciful tale of ghosts, often typified by stories of chain rattlings and moaning, Miss Despard's record is still one of the most objective and carefully written accounts about a haunted house in the literature of the field. A medical student at the time, Miss Despard eventually qualified as a physician. When one thinks of the social role of women of that era, Rose Despard must have been a rather remarkable young lady.

The family of Captain F. W. Despard moved into their quaint, multistoried dwelling in April 1882. It was in June that Rose Despard first sighted the apparition. While preparing for bed she thought she heard someone at the door, but upon investigation she saw no one. She proceeded into the hallway and saw "the figure of a tall lady, dressed in black, standing at the head of the stairs." With what must have taken considerable composure, Miss Despard began to follow the phantom but had to stop when her candle burned out. She also noted that the figure had a handkerchief over her face. This was to become one of the main characteristics of the ghost.

The figure was also seen in daylight in the garden, and several members of the family heard the eerie patter of footsteps. Between 1882 and 1884 Rose Despard saw the figure about six times. Also during this same period three other witnesses saw the phantasm. Rose's sister saw it in the summer of 1882 and thought it to be a Sister of Mercy, whom she described as "a tall black figure." In 1883 a maid saw the form and thought someone had broken into the house. In December 1883, Rose's little brother and a playmate saw a weeping woman which puzzled them.

Miss Despard must have had a scientific curiosity for she soon began to "experiment" with the ghost. How different from most families, who think only of ridding themselves of such unwanted visitors. An earthly nuisance is annoying enough, a supernatural one might well be unbearable.

On January 29, 1884, Miss Despard attempted her first experiment at communicating with the spirit. "I opened the drawing-room door softly and went in, standing just by it. She came in past me and walked to the sofa and stood still there, so I went up to her and asked her if I could help her. She moved, and I thought she was going to speak, but she only gave a slight gasp and moved towards the door. Just by the door I spoke to her again, but she seemed as if she were unable to speak. She walked into the hall, then by the side door she seemed to disappear as before."

Later that year Miss Despard experimented by tying strings across the stairs, but these strings were never upset by the specter and she even saw the shade glide through them.

After these initial experiences the apparition appeared more frequently. On one occasion, the ghost walked into the drawing room while Rose Despard was there reading a book in the company of her father and her sisters, but no one but Rose saw her. However, another time the apparition was seen by an independent witness, Mrs. K. "On the evening of August 11 (1884) we were sitting in the drawing room, with the gas lit but the shutters not shut, the light outside getting dusk, my brother and a friend having just given up tennis, finding it too dark, my eldest sister, Mrs. K. and myself both saw the figure on the balcony outside, looking in at the window. She stood there some minutes, then walked to the end and back again, after which she seemed to disappear. She soon after came into the drawing room, where I saw her, but my sister did not. That same evening my sister E. saw her on the stairs as she came out of a room on the upper landing."

The appearances became sporadic and it seemed that the figure was doomed to evaporate into the same mysterious unknown which had given it birth. From 1887 to 1889 the sightings became rare although its footsteps could still be heard. But even these faded away like the phantom form.

Who was this tall figure in black, weeping into her handkerchief? It seems that there is some evidence that the ghost was that of Imogene Swinhoe, the wife of the house's first tenant, who died tragically from the effects of chronic alcoholism. During an impromptu experiment Rose Despard attempted to pick out a photograph that resembled the phantom from a handful of random portraits. The one chosen by this clever young medical student turned out to be that of Imogene Swinhoe's sister, to whom she bore a strong family resemblance.

Phantoms are mysterious things. And in psychical research mystery breeds mystery. In the Cheltenham haunting one puzzling feature is that although the figure was solid enough to be mistaken for a living woman it was immaterial enough to pass through string and to be seen by some but not all those present. For some unknown reason Rose Despard had the sensitivity of perception to see the form continually, while the other members of the household were gifted with this faculty on only rare occasions.

If one looks for reasons or explanations, psychical phenomena will soon catapult the seeker into a quagmire. Unlike the inhabitants of our securely physical world (or the domain of our physical sensations) psychic phenomena do not follow the laws of physics or perception conveniently. It is of little value to try to fathom the mystery of why apparitions behave the way they do, or by what arcane guidelines we may be allowed to see them. In fact, some apparitions occasionally miss their mark, so to speak, and in one case, reported in *Phantasms of the Living,* a nursemaid saw an apparition trying to contact her mistress, who was oblivious to the whole episode. The maid described the phantom to her mistress, who was shocked, since the description fitted her brother, who shortly after was found to have been killed at the same time his apparition was seen. In this incident, the target was missed. A completely disinterested party became the relay for this dimension in human communication.

So it would appear that it is not everyone who is granted the great adventure of glimpsing the unknown. Only certain individuals have the ability to perceive the psychical. Perhaps this is for the best, for one can imagine the chaos in which we would find ourselves if we could no longer differentiate between sense perception, nonverbal communication, and psychic communication.

An experience of phantoms need not be only a visual one, for psychic perception is not franchised by the sense of sight alone. Phantasmal sounds, spectral odors, and even physical contact have been recorded. Yet, these feelings of an undefined and indescribable presence are every bit as real as the ghostly figures that have evoked man's curiosity for centuries.

Psychoanalysts often tell us that lurking beneath our sophisticated veneer we still maintain a primitive mental make-up which leads to a magical way of looking at the universe. The childhood world of fantasies, demons, and devils still hides beneath the façade of the human personality.

Jung was one of the first men to devote himself to the study of psychoanalysis. He shared the belief that the mind can create fantasies of the supernatural which have given rise to man's belief in unnatural creatures. Jung called these archetypal phantoms, engendered by the always active id, "exteriorized effects of unconscious complexes." In other words, projections from our own minds. While accepting the evidence of ESP, Jung could not tolerate the thought of other-world beings. This was in 1919, when he delivered his famous paper "The Psychological Foundations of Belief in Spirits" to the SPR. However, in 1947, commenting on this same paper, he added, "After collecting psychological experiences from among people and many countries for fifty years, I no longer feel as certain as I did in 1919. . . . To put it bluntly, I doubt whether an exclusively psychological approach can do justice to the phenomena in question."

What led Jung, master of the mind, to begin to feel that experiences with the occult might be more than just the projections of our own primitive thought processes? Like all the people whose personal anecdotes have been chronicled in this chapter, Jung's intrinsic understanding of the mind, his grasp of how the human personality thinks and is motivated, did not bar him from experiencing the supernormal himself. However, unlike the simple meeting of a specter on a staircase or beside a bed reported by so many, Jung's experience was more complex. For beneath his taut psychoanalytical veneer, Jung was also mystical. Like Rose Despard and hundreds of other individuals around the world, something in Jung's mental make-up or perceptual ability granted him power to experience psychic occurrences and all through his life he was pitched into brushes with the unexplained. These experiences puzzled him and even strained his relationship with his mentor, Sigmund Freud.

The most bizarre of Jung's apparitional adventures was in 1916 and led to his writing the rather esoteric script "Seven Sermons to the Dead." In his report on the occurrences Jung chronicled that the atmosphere of his home was thick with foreboding. One of his daughters had seen a white figure in the house and another daughter had had her bedclothes snatched away. The next day came the dramatic climax: "Around five o'clock in the afternoon on Sunday, the front doorbell began ringing frantically. It was a bright summer day; the two maids were in the kitchen, from which the open square outside the front door could be seen. Everyone immediately looked to see who was there but there was no one in sight. I was sitting near the doorbell, and not only heard it but saw it moving. We all simply stared at one another. The atmosphere was thick, believe me! Then I knew that something had to happen. The whole house was filled as if there were a crowd present, crammed full of spirits. They were packed deep right up to the door, and the air was so thick it was scarcely possible to breathe. As for myself, I was all aquiver with the question, 'For God's sake, what in the world is this?' "

Jung's outcry was the beginning of a strange document for, intuitively or psychically, he was answered by the "dead" and his reply became "Seven Sermons to the Dead." Who were these phantoms that so coerced Jung? Even the great thinker could not decide. He was a man broken into two—a psychoanalyst diagnosing his experience as a great upsurge of the unconscious projected beyond the bounds of the human mind and a psychic seeing these presences as a glimpse into the beyond.

As was said earlier, apparitions show little discrimination. Whether one chooses to believe in them or disbelieve matters not, for apparitions have appeared to both. Whether one is a naïve country housewife whose intellect is more keyed to doing household chores than pondering the mysteries of the mind, or a great psychoanalyst who daily explores the inner avenues of the unconscious, no immunity is granted.

An apparition may appear at any time or place—in one's home, on the street, or while visiting with friends. An apparition might also be recognized as someone who is alive, dead, dying, or it might remain a mystery—an unidentified form which appears and disappears fleetingly as though it were just as interested in getting a glimpse of us as we of it. Even our household pets can get no vaccination against the apparitional experience and apparitions may be seen singly or in groups.

Minot Savage once quoted a case which well typifies the mysterious mechanics of phantasmic appearances. The subject, a young woman, was playing a piano. Only her pet dog was with her. Suddenly the dog sat up growling. The young woman followed the dog's eyes to see three phantom forms. The forms melted away, while the dog, not as brave as its mistress, crouched beneath a couch. A safer vantage point, no doubt.

However, so far, we have really concentrated on but a few types of phantoms. Phantoms are complex and to list only a few other different types we might add: phantoms that proved their identity by revealing facts about themselves; phantoms with a mission; phantom faces; fiery phantoms; invisible phantoms; and many, many more.

When the question is asked, "Do you believe in ghosts?" the answer is not as simple as might be suspected. For that simple cliché-bound question is a launching pad into a world of the mysterious, far beyond the systematic day-to-day events to which we are all accustomed.

TWO

the return from silence

On October 11, 1907, Mrs. Rosa Sutton received a letter from her son, James, a lieutenant at Annapolis. The letter was a typical one that a rather homesick son writes to his parents—asking about brothers and sisters, reporting on his progress, conveying best wishes, and his outlook for the future. The Suttons were an average, middle-class American family living in Portland, Oregon. Mrs. Sutton was a housewife with several children. They were a proud family with a natural pride in having sent a son to Annapolis.

Although Jimmie's letter of October 11 was full of youthful vigor and good spirits, Mrs. Sutton knew something was wrong. The next evening, while busying herself with housework and family affairs, she suddenly had an attack of pain, a feeling of shock. She was so troubled that she bolted upstairs muttering that something was wrong with Jimmie.

Her feelings of distress continued. The next day she attended Mass, but that did not alter her uneasy sensations about her son. That day was the beginning of one of the most persistently appearing apparitions in the history of psychical research.

Mr. Sutton was called to the phone after his wife had returned from Mass. As he hung up to return to his work, Mrs. Sutton turned to her daughter, Louise. "Jimmie is here," she said. Her puzzled daughter replied, "Last night you said Jimmie was dead and now you say he is here." Mrs. Sutton insisted that her son was present and Louise finally gave in. To humor her mother she left her to prepare for Jimmie's arrival.

The joys of family reunion were soon shattered. Louise called to her mother that her father was home, distressed, pale, and faint.

"Can you stand some bad news?" asked Mr. Sutton.

"I can stand anything, anything except bad news from Jimmie."

"It is bad news and it is about Jimmie."

Mrs. Sutton hesitantly asked if her son were sick or injured. The news was tragic: Mr. Sutton had received a telegram informing them that their son had shot himself and was dead.

Mrs. Sutton could not believe that her son died by his own hand. Both of Mrs. Sutton's psychic impressions were correct: Jimmie was dead—but also present.

"At that instant," wrote Mrs. Sutton, "Jimmie stood right before me and said, 'Mamma, I never killed myself . . . my hands are as free from blood as when I was five years old.' "

No one else saw or heard anything, but Mrs. Sutton insisted her son was with them and her family thought that the shock of Jimmie's death was too hard an emotional blow for her to handle. Although they tried to calm her and talk her out of her vision, the apparition was persistent and continued to speak: ". . . a man hit me on the head with a butt of a gun so that I fell on my knees; then three of them jumped on me and beat me worse than a dog in the street and tried to run my face in the ground. They broke my watch with a kick as I lay on the ground. They jumped on me with their feet and I wonder that my ribs were not broken. I did not know that I was shot until my soul went to eternity. Oh, Mamma, if you could see my forehead, and put your hand on my forehead you would know what they did to me." Draped in his overcoat, the apparition began to vanish. "Mamma, don't lose your mind because you have got to clear my name."

This was not Mrs. Sutton's first encounter with the unknown. All her life she had had premonitions and telepathic experiences. Even her skeptical husband admitted to George Thacher, who investigated the case on behalf of Professor James Hyslop of the ASPR, that on several occasions his wife had revealed information that she could not have normally known. On one occasion Mrs. Sutton turned to her husband and stated, "Something has happened to Albert." Albert was her brother and it was later learned that he had indeed died at that time.

Some years before the family's move to Portland she had seen an apparition of her mother. The apparition revealed that she had died in Portland while visiting another daughter. Later that day a telegram arrived verifying the death. Luckily, Mrs. Sutton had already given the details of her mother's death to her husband, who was able to write out a corroborative statement for Thacher.

Unlike most apparitions that appear once and vanish forever, the phantom of Lieutenant Sutton was persistent. On October 16, when the Suttons still had not recovered from their shock, his form again appeared to his mother and gave further details about his death. "They put a bandage around my forehead and around to the back of my neck to try to hide what they had done. My face was all beaten up and discolored and my forehead broken and a lump under my left jaw. They put my body in a basement and left it there. . . . Utley managed and directed the whole affair." The wraith still appeared wrapped in an overcoat. It kept looking for something: "It's my shoulder knot that I can't find."

Later the apparition appeared and showed itself with its horribly disfigured face. The atmosphere in the Sutton home was alive with a psychic presence. Daisy, Jimmie's sister, dreamed the day after the family received the tragic news that someone showed her a face. Later, the girl identified the face from a portrait the family received—it was a fellow lieutenant, Utley.

"On the evening of the day on which my sister Mrs. Parker started from our home in Portland for Annapolis, which was on the 14th of October, 1907, the day after we heard of Jimmie's death," reported Daisy Sutton, "I was lying down in my room and whether I was asleep or not there seemed to be a haze in the room and I saw an arm holding a cabinet photograph before me and I got the impression of someone saying to me, 'there is the picture of the man who was most interested in directing the fight that killed Jimmie.' . . . Some days later the Army and Navy Register . . . was sent to my mother and she called my attention to a picture printed in that number of fourteen officers and student officers of the Marine Corps—my brother Jimmie was in the group . . . I . . . recognized at the lower right corner the face I had seen on the photograph in my dream, if it was a dream. My mother looked at the name under the picture and told me that the name of the officer I had recognized was Lieutenant Utley. . . .''

Three weeks after Jimmie's death his sister returned from the funeral at Annapolis, bringing with her the young man's belongings. These belongings were the first indication that the details given by the apparition could be verified, for as the phantom had stated, the crystal of his watch had been shattered.

For several months the apparition persistently appeared and finally the Suttons contacted James H. Hyslop. Hyslop had begun his career as a scholar and philosopher. A professor of ethics at Columbia University he was a self-avowed materialist. However, as with so many questioning savants before and after him, Hyslop was strangely attracted to the infant science of psychical research. At the time the Society for Psychical Research's work was becoming more and more controversial as more and more evidence for the existence of everything from telepathy to communication with the dead was collected. An American society was founded but soon merged with the London society. It sent out Dr. Richard Hodgson, who had decided to devote his life to psychical research, to take charge of the American research. Hyslop and Hodgson became acquainted, Hyslop as an eager student, Hodgson as a somewhat pompous and reticent, though patient and severe, mentor.

Hodgson was studying the phenomenal abilities of the Boston medium Mrs. Leonore Piper, who would go into trance, and while in that state personalities alleged to be the dead would communicate with her. Far from conveying the banal, platitudinous messages that usually compose the repertoire of ''spirit messages,'' these personalities had given their names, details of their lives and relationships in such detail that it would have been impossible for Mrs. Piper to have obtained this information about people, dead and alive, who were total strangers to her. Mrs. Piper had been sent to England to be studied by European savants. Hodgson soon became convinced that these ''communicators'' were in fact surviving personalities of the dead. Many British researchers also were converted to a belief in life after death through this Boston sensitive.

James Hyslop was also converted from his materialistic precepts by Mrs. Piper, for after several sittings which he had anonymously with the medium, he was confronted by personalities communicating through the entranced woman that identified themselves as Hyslop's deceased relatives, gave their correct names, and incidents of their lives the only record of which was the personal recollections of Hyslop himself. After these sittings, Hyslop wrote a huge report on them and later gave up his professorship to devote full time to psychical research.

In 1905 Richard Hodgson collapsed during a handball game—dead from heart failure. Hyslop, now the leading researcher in the United States, took over the reins of the American Society for Psychical Research and instituted it as a separate body from the London society. He edited the *Proceedings* and *Journal* of the organization, became its principal spokesman and research officer, as well as main contributor to its publications. He carried on this monumental task until his death in 1920.

Mrs. Sutton wrote Hyslop on October 5, 1910. The apparition of her son was still plaguing her, although she found great satisfaction in his appearances. She had been robbed of her son, but not of his presence. Since Hyslop was in New York and the Suttons in Oregon, he could not personally investigate. Instead he sent a friend, George Thacher, to call upon the Suttons and furnish the report. By now the Suttons had verified much of what the apparition had revealed, but this is getting ahead of the story.

When the parents were first notified of their son's death, the telegram merely read, "It is reported from Annapolis Lieut. James N. Sutton committed suicide at 1:20 this morning October 13th 1907." It was at this time that Mrs. Sutton saw her son's phantom, which acquainted her with several facts about his death. These details she told her husband.

The official story that led the inquest to declare the death a suicide was as follows: According to the report the incident began at a Naval dance. After the affair Lieutenant Sutton and some buddies started to drive back to camp. During their drive a fight broke out between Sutton and a couple of his fellow officers, during which the lieutenant was thrown to the ground. He threatened to kill his antagonists before morning and returned to his tent to obtain two pistols. This led to his arrest and during the attempt to seize him he began to fire. He was knocked down and beaten during the melée and suddenly deliberately shot himself. He was presumably drunk during the entire incident.

Although the story was accepted, a lot of questions needed to be answered. As Hyslop pointed out, several points could be argued against the story: (1) There was no motivation stated for the initial fight. (2) There was no information about what occurred between the two fights. Further, all this evidence came from those who were involved in the quarrel and death. (3) There was no intelligible reason why Sutton would have killed himself. (4) The testimonies of the witnesses were inconsistent. (5) The possibility of homicide was never considered.

This is all that the Suttons had to go on. But the apparition still maintained its activity. In 1909 the Suttons had the body, which had been interred at Arlington Cemetery, exhumed. On examination of the remains more of Mrs. Sutton's suspicions were confirmed. For although the Navy doctors had sworn at the inquest that the Lieutenant's face was not disfigured, the body showed that the boy's forehead had been battered and that a lump, formed by injuries, was under his chin. This corresponded exactly to what the apparition had revealed: "My face was all beaten up and discolored and my forehead broken and a lump under my left jaw." Apparently it also was true that Sutton's body was placed in a basement at one time and the shoulder knot about which the apparition complained was missing.

We will never know the truth about Lieutenant Sutton's death. It was suggestive, however, that the report of the autopsy clearly stated that the angle of the bullet's entry into the body and the nature of the wound were inconsistent with the suicide hypothesis.

One thing is sure, though. Before any official news from Annapolis had arrived Mrs. Sutton knew her son was dead. She saw his apparition, which described, and later showed, some of its wounds which were not verified until after the body was exhumed. These injuries were in contradiction to the official inquest report. Finally the apparition gave the name of his alleged murderer, a name that correctly indicated someone who was intricately involved in the death. As for the official inquest report, Hyslop summed it up: "The examination of the body after exhumation two years later showed wounds and conditions which had no proper consideration in the earlier inquest and the direction of the bullet, as also shown in the original autopsy, was against the theory of suicide as testified, and the direct testimony of some witnesses made it appear impossible.'' In fact, no one actually saw the alleged suicide. The incident occurred at night and all that was seen and heard was a flash of a gun and a shot. It was only inferred that the young officer was his own victim.

Certainly then, the apparition's story is just as plausible and more consistent than the report. The Suttons never solved the case conclusively. No further investigations could really reopen the case, and so it remains an unsolved mystery.

George Thacher turned out to be a more than able investigator. Interviewing the Suttons, he was able to verify most of Mrs. Sutton's claims. Not only did several family members acknowledge the accuracy of Mrs. Sutton's apparitional visions, but friends as well had known of her reports before the family started to verify their deceased son's story. A cousin, Mary Hodgson, told Thacher that she distinctly remembered Mrs. Sutton telling her that her son claimed to have been injured on the forehead and under the jaw. Dorothy Hincks was a friend who had rushed to comfort the distressed woman when she heard of the family's bereavement. She too remembered that the mother told her that the lieutenant's apparition had appeared and complained of being beaten to the ground and then shot.

The apparition said it had had a bandage tied about its head concealing a wound. Wounds on the scalp and forehead were found when the body was exhumed. Chrissie Hincks, another friend of the Suttons, testified that Mrs. Sutton told her that the apparition said ''there's a hole underneath the bandage on my forehead.'' All told, there were over ten witnesses to Mrs. Sutton's story.

Thacher also spent considerable time perusing all the official reports. It was he who discovered important discrepancies in the inquest report. Thacher also discovered that Sutton seemed conscious of the fact that his life would soon end. A month before his death he took out a life insurance policy and only a week or so before the shooting he wrote home, ''I feel in my bones something is going to happen, but it is the feeling most people laugh at.''

Not only did Thacher find that Mrs. Sutton had continually seen the apparition, but several other members of the family had strange experiences about the time of the officer's death. The deceased's brother, Dan, saw the phantom. His sister, Louise, had felt the boy's presence. A mystery was being uncovered.

When there was a puzzle to be solved James Hyslop would often enlist the aid of a psychic in hope that someone more attuned to extrasensory perceptions would be able to either independently corroborate the claims of those reporting a psychic influence or procure further evidence or details.

Thacher also thought this was a worthwhile endeavor and with the aid of a friend, a medium named Mrs. Youmans, set up sittings to see if further details could be elicited via an extrasensory channel.

Mrs. Youmans was unaware of the Suttons' experience but at the first sitting the sensitive seemed to pick up the horrible story, obtaining vivid impressions of a death. "Somebody hit me in the head here [pointing to the back of her head]. Somebody hit me on the chin and cracked me on the ground—Somebody killed somebody—Such a nice boy." More impressions came to the sensitive: "There's trees but it's dark; it's not so very dark. Revolver, oh, I wish I had not said revolver. . . ." "Right back of me there's a tent and a tree close. They did—two of them did. Both are equally guilty. One was afraid and went away. The other he went about his business—he sneered at it. There's no drinking like it was said."

These impressions were given after Mrs. Youmans had been given a sealed letter. Opening the letter, Thacher found it to be an anonymously written note to the Suttons that stated that their son had been murdered and did not commit suicide. The handwriting was not disguised and apparently matched that of a young serviceman who was at the scene of the crime. Hyslop tried to trace the witness but failed.

After the body had been exhumed and the phantom's testimony verified, Mrs. Sutton saw less and less of her son's apparition. It too remained, like its death, an enigma.

Just as important as verifying that Mrs. Sutton really did see an apparition is the natural question What was the apparition? Was it the surviving personality of Lieutenant Sutton?

While psychical research has more facts than explanations,

parapsychologists are often grouped into two categories. One group is the "survivalists." Like Hyslop and Hodgson, these researchers feel that the evidence amassed by psychical research, especially phenomena such as mediumship and apparitions, points not only to man's ability to survive death but also to his ability to contact those who are still living. The other group is the "anti-survivalists." Since ESP has no known limits, they argue, the mind has access to all information via ESP, thus gaining any data it may need telepathically and clairvoyantly. This being so, it is not necessary to postulate that any information comes from the dead.

How would these two different approaches explain the Lieutenant Sutton case?

Anti-survivalists would claim that Mrs. Sutton could not accept her son's suicide. After all, the family was Roman Catholic and suicide is a mortal sin. Through her ESP she was able to reconstruct the actual scene either through clairvoyance or telepathy from those who were at the scene. This augmented her extrasensory awareness that her son had died. Gathering these ESP impressions, she unconsciously projected an apparition.

The survivalists will object strenuously to this theory. They would rightly point out that not only did Mrs. Sutton have these experiences, but other members of the family also had similar experiences. Are we to believe that the entire family was psychic?

The survivalistic viewpoint does offer a good explanation for the continual appearance of the phantom. First, Lieutenant Sutton as a Catholic would have great motivation to return to his family to remove the stigma of suicide and see justice done. It is an old tradition that ghosts and hauntings are initiated by a tragedy and there is good evidence to support this claim. G. W. Lambert, who has written widely on parapsychology, has criticized this belief on the grounds that "it is a relic of superstition, and should not be encouraged . . ." Then why doesn't Mr. Lambert offer any support for his claims? In fact, there is a mass of evidence in support of this "superstition." Ernesto Bozzano in his book *Les phénomènes de hantise* found that in 80 percent of over three hundred cases of haunting phenomena, a tragedy was involved which led to the manifestations. Lieutenant Sutton's ghost is in good company it seems.

There is also evidence that those who have died are very worried when their deaths are attributed to suicide. The following is a typical and famous case, verified and published by the SPR.

"Some thirty-five years ago," writes Mr. D., "I took into my employment a tender delicate-looking boy, Robert MacKenzie, who was in dire straits, being literally homeless and starving. He worked for me for a number of years and always evidenced an intensity of gratitude."

Years later Mr. D. moved away and hardly thought about his former employee. But one night as he lay in that borderline between sleep and waking he seemed to be involved in a business transaction: "Toward me, in front, advanced Robert MacKenzie, and feeling annoyed, I addressed him with some asperity, asking him if he did not see that I was engaged, . . . 'I must speak to you at once . . . I wish to tell you, sir, that I am accused of doing a thing I did not do, and that I want *you* to know it, and to tell you so, and that you are to forgive me for what I am blamed for, because I am innocent.' "

When D. awoke, his wife rushed in with the news that MacKenzie had killed himself by drinking poison. Later however the manager who had dispatched the news admitted he was in error. The lad had drunk a glass of poison thinking it was whisky and soon died.

Was this a telepathic impression from the dying boy? Did the boy even know that it was thought he had committed suicide? Or did he somehow transcend death to assure his former employer of his innocence? Much the same problem exists as with the restless phantom of Lieutenant Sutton.

How one wishes to explain the psychic manifestations that plagued Mrs. Sutton for over two years will depend on whether one believes in survival of death or not.

But one thing is certain. Mrs. Sutton's experiences are inexplicable unless we admit to some form of extrasensory perception. Whether it was her own psychical abilities that initiated her visions or whether it was the motivation of her dead, yet surviving son is a problem that has not been resolved in psychical research up to now.

THREE

brushes with the unseen

As the bizarre experiences of C. G. Jung show, a phantom need not appear to the visual senses in order to indicate its presence. Often, instead of a phantasmal appearance itself, other inexplicable occurrences might manifest. There is almost an infinite variety of psychical effects that can excite one or more of our senses. The senses of hearing, feeling, smelling, and, on rare occasions, even tasting have been stirred into action by a psychic stimulus.

The sense of hearing is a common psychic perception. Captain A. W. Monckton was fortunate, or unfortunate, enough to have missed the opportunity of seeing a phantom. But he certainly heard it. Monckton was a magistrate in New Guinea and chronicled his adventure in his autobiographical *Some Experiences of a New Guinea Resident Magistrate*. The strangeness of the events only added to the strangeness of that half-wild country. As Captain Monckton's story goes, he was alone, staying in the house of a friend. Carrying out his official business in the flimsily built abode, he suddenly was struck by the fact that the doors leading to a veranda which had been securely closed were now standing open.

"As I wrote," the Captain narrated, "I became conscious that both doors were wide open, and—hardly thinking what I was doing—I got up, closed them both, and went on writing. A few minutes later, I heard footsteps upon the coral path leading up to the house; they came across the squeaky palm veranda, my door opened, and the footsteps went across the room and—as I raised my eyes from my dispatch—the other door opened, and the footsteps passed across the veranda and down again on to the coral.''

Rationalizing to himself that one of the servants had scurried through the room but that his eye had not caught him, he closed the doors and once again occupied himself with his business. But Monckton was disturbed once more: ''Some time later, once more the footsteps came, crash crash on the coral, squeak squeak on the veranda; again my door opened and the squeak changed to the tramp of booted feet on the boarded floor. As I looked to see who it was, the tramp passed close behind my chair and across the room to the door, which opened, and then again the tramp changed to the squeak and the squeak to the crash on the coral.''

Captain Monckton described himself, euphemistically no doubt, as ''puzzled.'' He tried to convince himself that his mind was playing tricks, but a third repetition of the events finally prompted the magistrate to initiate an investigation. Calling in the servants, he made a search, although I am sure the servants were not quite sure what they were looking for. However, I am also certain that they were stunned by what happened next. As they all were together in the room, ''Presently, exactly the same thing occurred once more. Through the line of men came the footsteps; through my room in precisely the same manner came the tread of a heavily-booted man, then went on to the palm veranda, where—in the now brilliant illumination—we could *see the depressing at the spots from which the sound came,* as though a man were stepping there.''

The Captain never could explain what had disturbed him, and his narrative reports that he slept aboard ship for the rest of the night.

These experiences bring to mind another phantom that did not need to appear to make its presence known. My colleague, Raymond Bayless, had a similar experience while investigating a purported haunted house in the Eagle Rock section of Los Angeles. As he reported it, he was having coffee with the tenant of the house when he heard the front door open. The tenant explained that it was only ''the ghost'' making the noise and not to be disturbed about it. Mr. Bayless really didn't take the remark seriously but on going to the door, ''I quickly realized that the door in reality had not opened at all. It was in plain sight as I listened to the sounds of it closing, and it was obviously tightly closed. As I walked within a few feet of the door I heard three distinct footsteps walk away from the door into the carpeted hallway. In spite of the carpeting the footsteps were very audible. They were within my immediate range of vision. There was no doubt that the walker was completely invisible. There was simply nothing to see."

Even taste and touch have been affected by the psychic. One woman quoted in *Phantasms of the Living* reported how she felt a blow to her face and tasted blood at the same time her husband was similarly injured aboard a boat.

Unseen presences can be just as vivid and real as those that show themselves to us, The wide range of experiences with invisible phantoms came dramatically to a head when I personally found myself with a box seat to a psychic drama.

It is rare that a researcher finds himself in the middle of an active haunted house. Rarer yet, to find himself occupying a haunted house. It is unfortunately true that most people who have experienced hauntings are not good witnesses to the occurrences, nor are they sufficiently aware of psychical research to evaluate them. It was by some unbelievably good fortune that I was able to observe two series of haunting outbreaks when I moved into a surburban house in Los Angeles.

The house is an old Spanish-style two-bedroom and den house in Canoga Park, a suburb of Los Angeles. The first occupants who lived there were two friends of mine, Carlos Romero and Dennis Jones, both in their early twenties. I had known both for a long time and, in fact, immediately before they moved into the house in February 1971, the three of us had shared a large apartment a few miles away.

About six months later Carlos casually remarked to me that he had encountered some strange happenings in the house. Sometimes he heard the front screen door opening; records mysteriously disappeared from the record cabinet only to reappear later; objects were moved into different positions when no one was in the house; and two dogs had been found inside the house after they had been locked outside.

A third tenant of the house was Marc F., who also moved into the house in June 1971. Carlos told me that Marc had noticed odd disappearances of things. When I talked to him about it he verified that "odd things" occurred in the house. Interestingly enough, Carlos reported to me that the effects began soon after they had removed a chimney flue. Dennis also remarked that after the removal of the flue the house "felt strange." I wouldn't have put too much stock into this had it not been that Carlos had not told Dennis his impression until *after* Dennis had remarked about his feelings to him.

Since the testimony did seem suggestive I made several visits to the house. During these visits only one odd incident took place. One evening in June 1971 when Carlos and I were in the kitchen we both definitely heard the front screen door open and shut. Unfortunately we could not verify the whereabouts at that time of a dog and a cat who also shared the house (on an equal basis) with the tenants.

In December 1971 I moved into the house after all the tenants but Carlos had moved out. Nothing at all abnormal occurred until April 1972. Quite honestly I had really forgotten that I was supposed to be living in a haunted house which I had moved into because of convenience not because of my investigations. I had long felt that, all in all, malobservation, tricks of memory, etc., usually are the true explanations of hauntings and that this house was probably no exception.

Something, however, had quite a different attitude.

On the evening of April 16, I arrived back at the house, after visiting some friends, at about two o'clock in the morning. The next morning Carlos told me of a strange and frightening experience he had the night before which he wrote out for my files:

> While in my bedroom studying the first movement of the Tchaikovsky Violin Concerto [looking it over, not practicing it], I did experience something that I thought I might have imagined. The outcome of this experience turned out to be very real, not an hallucination. On this particular evening my co-tenant [myself] was visiting some friends. My Great Dane and I were the only ones in the house. The dog was chewing her bone in the middle room of our house which looks into our living room. About 9:30 P.M. while in my bedroom I heard our screen door along with the wooden door slam shut [both doors were closed and locked at the time]. Then I heard about four or five footsteps. I thought

nothing of it because I just thought it was Scott coming home. When my dog began to bark furiously I knew something was wrong since she never barks at him when he enters. My thoughts were that somebody had broken in. I went to see who it was, and to my surprise I found nobody. My dog continued to stare and bark at the doorway.

I might add that the reaction of the dog was truly odd. Despite the fact that we had tried to train her as a watchdog, unexpected visitors coming up on the porch were usually greeted with furious tail-wagging or indifference.

Carlos told me this incident the next morning and remarked that he had been pretty well shaken up over it. The next day (April 18) he told me of another episode which he also wrote up. "On April 17, 1972 at around 2:30 A.M. [actually it was on the 18th, the night of the 17th] I was awakened by some unusual sounds. I was asleep in my room when I was awakened by some humming. This humming came in three different groups. There were three hums per group. In all, there were a total of nine hummings. They always began low in pitch and the vibrations were very wide. As the pitch of the hummings got higher the intensity of the vibrations began to tighten up—the thing about these hummings is that I couldn't locate from which direction they were coming."

The day before Carlos reported his odd experience I had begun to have a few myself. I was taking an afternoon nap when suddenly it felt as though something had jumped onto the bed. I thought it might be our cat, but this was not the case. I didn't think much of the occurrence until the same jolting recurred the next two days. I then realized, after what Carlos had reported to me, that these effects might have a psychic cause. The bouncing, which became so powerful as to literally shake the entire bed, always occurred in the afternoon, and the force always pushed from the bottom of the bed. It was not caused by muscle quirks that often accompany the onset of sleep. I am most aware of this phenomenon and my experiences were of a different nature entirely.

The most startling experience of this kind occurred on April 22. By this time I had checked the springs, the mattress, and the frame of the bed. I went to bed at midnight and consciously lay willing the "force" to bounce the bed. Fifteen minutes later, while I was fully awake and perfectly still, something jerked and bounced the bed. This was the fourth incident of this kind and the first that occurred at night. On this occasion the "force" pushed down, striking the bed right next to my head. The reverberations were so strong that the bed shook for a few seconds. I was absolutely still at the time, awake, and very startled. After this episode the bed was shaken a few more times at different hours, once before I got out of bed in the morning, but the shakings became weaker and weaker and finally stopped altogether.

Although the phantom force had apparently given up on me, Carlos was still having some weird experiences. On the morning of April 24 he was awakened at 3:40 A.M. by a crisp, stinging sound. After this sound had manifested he very clearly heard low moanings coming from the wall adjoining his bed. These moans lasted about a minute. By chance I was also awake in my room at the time. I heard nothing and our dog quietly slept in the kitchen where she stays during the night.

On the morning of April 26 my bed was violently shaken and rocked backwards and forwards for a few seconds. After this last outburst all manifestations ceased.

From my investigations I had determined that these effects come in groups and activate for a short period and then disappear for a long period of time, usually several months. This turned out to be the case, for in December 1973 we had a short but very dramatic series of events.

On December 26, I awoke at 3:20 A.M. A fierce wind was bellowing outside and I had a difficult time sleeping. I began to fall back to sleep again when all of a sudden I was wide awake and hearing what sounded like a single string of a violin being softly bowed. This sound was repeated, in my room, three times and was very distinct.

I didn't know what to make of this experience until the next day the wildest phenomena I have encountered really shook me up. Carlos was in the kitchen sweeping the floor and busying himself with cleaning. He had just been on the phone with an acquaintance of ours and I called out to Carlos, who was out of my vision, "What else did she have to say?" I heard a gruff male voice from the kitchen answer sarcastically and in a hoarse semi-whisper,

"Nothing—nothing—nothing." I walked into the kitchen to discover Carlos just coming into the house from the backyard. I asked him, "Were you talking to me or the dog?" He was very puzzled since he had been outside all the time and had not heard me call to him. Carlos, also a bit shaken, admitted to me that the night before while preparing for bed he had just turned off his stereo when he heard a very clear male voice say the single word "No."

What is so interesting is that when I classified all the incidents we had witnessed a definite pattern was obvious. Carlos and I usually had our independent experiences on alternating nights—one night he would have an unusual event and the next night it would be my turn.

Since then the house has been silent and I imagine it will be a few months before my next brush with the unseen.

My experiences and those of Captain Monckton and Mr. Bayless were basically auditory ones. Yet phantoms don't even have to be heard to manifest themselves. As with experiences such as Mrs. Hurth's, who just "knew" that her daughter had been hit by a car, psychic perceptions often seem independent of our physiological senses. Anne Bridge, the novelist, has aptly described psychic experiences as "moments of knowing" and this poetic description is very appropriate and concise.

Our senses are actually information sources that help us function in the world, gathering data for us to assemble so that we can recognize our surroundings. We judge our world by what we see, hear, feel, smell, and taste. Through years and years all the bits of information have been passed on to the brain, catalogued, and stored for future reference. Yet our awareness is not dependent on sense perceptions, for consciousness may be maintained without them. Experiments have been carried out in the strange realm of sensory deprivation where the subject is stripped of all his physical sensations. How does one react to such a state? Subjects have reported everything from vivid hallucinations to explorations into new dimensions of the mind.

Extrasensory perception, that faculty whereby we experience the unknown through phantoms, telepathy, clairvoyance, is really not perception at all. When a telepathic "vision" is seen, in most instances there is no physical sensation. What is in fact occurring is a process of information. The mind, somehow coming into contact with uncharted stimuli, reveals this data to the mind in the form of a "perception," usually visual. Since the physical senses are the only channel that we can exercise to receive incoming data, it is certainly not odd that the mind would trick the senses into revealing important information to the conscious mind.

Yet, experiences such as Mrs. Hurth's show that psychic perception can go beyond this limit and can be directly jolted into consciousness, bypassing the physical senses. These are very much "moments of knowing."

By the same token, experiencing a phantom presence need not appeal to physical sensations. Some persons have had experiences that were very real but beyond any rational sensory perception. It is almost as if one were able to sense a presence, to become intuitively aware that one is immediately in a strange and even frightening situation.

Hereward Carrington, a famous psychical researcher who died in 1958, reported a firsthand experience he and a group of investigators had while probing a haunted house. Carrington, it should be noted, was one of the most versatile and experienced investigators that psychical research ever produced. An indefatigable researcher, his years of investigation brought him into contact with such notable mediums as Eusapia Palladino, an Italian peasant woman, during whose séances tables would levitate and spectral hands would hit and nudge the experimenters. Carrington had an iron disposition and was one of the most critical investigators to rise above the dual impairments of childish credulity and irrational skepticism that have always strangled the study of psychical phenomena. Because of this, Carrington's odd reaction to this adventure, which no doubt began as a routine investigation, is all the more striking.

On the night of April 13, 1937 Carrington and his wife, also a seasoned investigator, led a team of seven participants to a reputedly haunted house outside New York City. Carrington had been told about the house by a former tenant who had complained of odd noises and an inability to retain his servants. Carrington, along with his wife, the former tenant, and four friends teamed up for a night in the house. They also brought along a dog that had lived in the house.

Using the traditional methods of investigating an alleged haunting, the group began by examining the residence room by room in order to assure themselves that no obvious normal explanation could be found for the sounds. The investigation was a blank until a few members of the team began to get feelings of apprehension, a vague but definite sensation that there was something odd about the place. Carrington suggested that they go to the upper floor which contained the servants' quarters, and he vividly described what happened when they attempted to search the little apartments:

> I could see that the top floor was brilliantly lighted, and that a steep flight of stairs lay just ahead of me. Leading the way, with the others close behind me, I ascended the stairs, and made a sharp turn to the right, finding myself confronted by a series of small rooms.
>
> The instant I did so, I felt as though a vital blow had been delivered to my solar plexus. My forehead broke out in profuse perspiration, my head swam, and I had difficulty swallowing. It was a most extraordinary sensation, definitely physiological, and unlike anything I had ever experienced before. A feeling of terror and panic seized me, and for the moment I had the utmost difficulty in preventing myself from turning and fleeing down the stairs! Vaguely I remember saying aloud, "Very powerful! Very powerful!"
>
> My wife, who was just behind me, had taken a step or two forward. She was just exclaiming, "Oh, what cute little rooms!" when the next moment she was crying "No! No!" and raced down the steep flight of stairs like a scared rabbit! (She had not run up or down stairs for more than two years because of an injury to her back, but she flew down the stairs and past those coming up after her without even seeing or touching them!)

This is surely a bizarre reaction for two psychical researchers who were long famous for exposing even the cleverest of fake mediums. Even though they both had numerous encounters with the unseen during other psychic explorations, these were invariably met with a calm and detached appraisal.

Carrington found his wife outside the house sitting on the porch trying to recuperate from her moment of terror. The other members of the team had similar negative experiences and one even came down the stairs weeping uncontrollably. Collecting their thoughts and reentering the house, the team, a few members of which had been skeptical and cynical about the whole matter, once again proceeded to investigate. They waited, expecting some psychic manifestation to explode but nothing happened. Again venturing into the forbidding upstairs quarters, the group experienced nothing abnormal whatsoever. The gloom, terror, and heavy atmosphere had vanished. At this time, the former tenant admitted that a suicide had died in those same upper rooms.

Not only did the investigators feel a great sense of relief, but the dog that accompanied them scurried up the stairs. Earlier in the evening he could not be coaxed up them, growling and bristling his hair all the while. After a few more routine procedures, the harrowing night in the haunted house came to an innocuous close. To the relief of the researchers, one may safely bet.

Carrington and his wife shared a further adventure with a somewhat transparent presence while he was delivering a lecture. All of a sudden he was attacked by giddiness and confusion which lasted until he walked to the other side of a table upon which rested his audiovisual aids. His head cleared, the talk resumed, and Carrington attributed the experience to faintness.

Oddly though, Carrington's wife had seen a grayish "cloud" around him at one point during the lecture which stayed stationary as Carrington pulled himself to the other side of the table. The auric-like shadow then disintegrated.

Psychologically, it would be easy to label Carrington's experience in the haunted house an anxiety reaction. All of us harbor unverbalized fear. Usually this fear is projected to something—as in phobias. But in other cases the fear finds no outlet and becomes free-floating, gradually building until it explodes into an attack of panic. The heartbeat increases, sweating is profuse, and the poor victim has no realization what exactly is causing it. Anxiety attacks are, however, not contagious and it would be necessary to go beyond this simplistic explanation to understand why seven psychologically independent people should all react with horror at the same time. Could it be that some attacks of panic, fear, or horror actually represent a reaction to a real, though intangible threat? Could in fact the pressure of some psychic embodiment prompt such a reaction?

Raymond Bayless, who has had a wide range of experience in dealing with the psychic during his twenty-five years as a psychical investigator shared one of these uncanny occurrences in 1938. At the time he was a teen-ager and he and his brother arrived one night at their home in Denver. No one was home and the two boys went into the house. While Raymond stayed downstairs his brother, Alan, went upstairs to lie down. Raymond suddenly became aware of an unnatural presence: "Suddenly for absolutely no reason that I was able to discover, I had an overwhelming impression that something frightful was in the house. So powerful was this feeling that I actually started to run for the back door." Dashing to get out of the house, he nearly collided with his brother, who had just raced down the stairs. The two made a beeline for the door. Composing himself, Alan reported that he too had had a sudden and inexplicable feeling that something horrible was in the house and that he had to flee from it.

I have often asked Raymond Bayless about this experience. Although he didn't know what to make of it, he and his brother were so frightened that they did not reenter the house for some time. When they finally did venture back, just as in Carrington's case, whatever had catalyzed their panic was gone.

No one could be better able to judge the difference between an anxiety attack and a psychical impression than a psychiatrist. But as with Jung, a life devoted to the understanding of the mind does not disqualify one from experiencing these psychologically inexplicable events.

Arthur Guirdham is a British psychiatrist who has spent much time thinking and writing about, as well as experiencing, the psychical. Like the Bayless brothers, he too experienced an unfathomable terror in the face of a paranormal presence, though in this case an actual phantom was seen. It might be expected that Dr. Guirdham, trained in the demanding discipline of psychiatry, would have found a psychological explanation for his reaction. But after all these years he still feels his experience was beyond any phenomenon with which psychiatry has ever come to grips: "As nearly as I can say I was six or seven. I was lying in bed when I felt drawn and horrified by a presence outside my bedroom. I rose from my bed . . . and opened the door to my room." Guirdham saw a frightful humanlike phantom. Terrified, he found himself going through a ritual of prayer, jumped into bed, then back to his knees praying in an obsessional manner. "I felt myself in the presence of great evil. I responded to evil not by guilt but by sheer naked panic."

Guirdham has also had psychical impressions as an adult. While on a mountain trip he suddenly had a great sense of repulsion and depression. Later he learned that his experience manifested while he was traversing a mountainous area where centuries ago a most brutal slaughter had occurred.

Animals also react bizarrely to invisible presences. By tradition dogs are supposed to cower in fear in haunted houses. Cats are supposed to arch their backs and hiss defiantly at some impression that has escaped our own physical senses. Such traditions seem to be well founded, as the dog brought by Carrington to the haunted house in New York indicated.

A few recent examples of this type have been outlined by Dr. Robert Morris, a psychologist who has had a long association as a researcher with the Psychical Research Foundation (PRF) in Durham, North Carolina. In one case a researcher he knew investigated a purported haunted house in Kentucky. Accompanying him, instead of the usual entourage of psychical investigators, was a dog, a cat, a rat, and a rattlesnake. One by one he placed these animals in the room, the site of a tragedy, where the haunting was reported to focus. The dog reacted by snarling and refused to stay in the room. Similarly, the cat hissed, leaped from the owner's arms, spitting at an unoccupied and otherwise innocuous chair. The rat had no reaction whatsoever. Perhaps it shared the parapsychologists' cool detachment and objective attitudes during research investigations. But the rattlesnake had a strong reaction. "It immediately assumed an attack posture focusing on the same chair that had been of interest to the cat. . . . When placed in another room of the house not linked with past tragedy, none of the four animals showed a noticeable response."

These anecdotal reports of odd animal behavior are consistent with some recent findings in experimental parapsychology. Since the 1930s just about the only absolute finding that parapsychology has made from experimental work has been that ESP is elusive, inconsistent, and only with the best of ESP subjects is it in the least repeatable. Those who saw in experimental parapsychology the road to the repeatable experiment were quickly disillusioned. While

ESP research with human subjects has not led to the type of invariability once dreamed of, experimentation with animals has opened up not only a new world of experimental designs and findings, but a higher level of consistency than with human subjects.

Back in 1924 a Russian researcher, V. Bechterev, was already experimenting with animals to see if dogs would respond to unspoken thoughts. Bechterev was president of the Psychoneurological Academy and director of the Institute for the Investigation of the Brain in St. Petersburg.

An-psi research, as ESP testing with animals has been labeled, has become a mainstay of research at the Foundation for Research on the Nature of Man (FRNM). This is the old Duke parapsychology lab which was reorganized when it moved off the Duke campus when its founder-director, J. B. Rhine, retired. This research in animal ESP successfully confirmed similar experiments carried out in France. In the French studies, mice seemed to be able, by precognition, to consistently avoid the one side of their cage which was about to be given an electrical shock. By chance, the mice should have avoided this unpleasant, though harmless shock only 50 percent of the time. When all the results were tabulated they showed that they avoided the shock successfully at chances of 1000 to 1.

In a paper delivered to the American Association for the Advancement of Science in 1971, Walter Levy and Anita McRae reported on seven experiments they had carried out trying to confirm the French experiments. Astoundingly, just about all the experiments significantly indicated that the animals were aware by the use of ESP of when they were about to be shocked. Since that time more and more experiments with animals have been attempted, many with success.

In the light of recent research findings, it is natural that animals would react to psi (psychic) impressions even if they bypass us. Parapsychologically speaking, there is sound anecdotal and experimental evidence to support the fact that animals are more consistent in their ability to be cognizant of psi than human beings. On a psychological level this is not odd either. The rarity of ESP impressions that come to consciousness suggests that psi impressions are automatically repressed from consciousness. We repress them, perhaps, because we do not believe in them, because they cause a disturbance to our set way of thinking. In short, they are anxiety-provoking. As is well known to psychology, a person will react in any way possible to eliminate anxiety. With ESP, we merely repress it. Animals, on the other hand, do not have our well-developed personalities and defense mechanisms. They probably are not bothered by the need to repress their ESP impressions.

Man is endowed with many avenues by which he contacts the outside world. While we have come to rely upon the world of physical sensation as the most accommodating way to function, we must not make the fatal error of refusing to admit to more subtle faculties which interplay on so camouflaged a level with our physical senses that we do not even recognize them. An interesting experiment along these lines was carried by Dr. Rex Stanford, a young experimental psychologist at the University of Virginia School of Medicine. It was Dr. Stanford's plan to try to show that even without conscious knowledge or volition, psychical impressions interplay with our daily sensory input.

Stanford's experiment was novel. Thirty young male subjects listened to a recording of a dream experience. Unknown to the subjects, the dream was a fabricated one, especially composed to intrigue the listeners. Individually each subject was quizzed about certain features of the dream by selecting one of four answers offered. The catch was that some of the questions asked had no correct answer given in the account. One would expect that on these questions the various subjects would randomly select from the different answers offered with little agreement in comparison to general agreement on those questions that did have solutions in the dream story. After the interviews were completed, "correct" answers to these trick questions were selected by the experimenters using a completely impartial method. Upon rechecking it was found that the subjects had inadvertently chosen the answers that were later chosen to be the correct ones. The odds were way above what could be expected by chance and even though the subjects were unaware of it, somehow some sort of extrasensory perception had interplayed with their memory causing them to become aware of the hypothetical correct answers even though they had no normal way of knowing them.

If Stanford's views are correct, and he has made a valiant attempt to obtain evidence for them, then every day we probably receive extrasensory perceptions (in telepathic or apparitional experiences as well) which although never fully reaching consciousness reflect on our behavior and interpersonal relationships.

It seems that although ESP often reaches us by tricking our sensory organs, ESP may also bypass them. In the experiences of Carrington in his weird haunted house, the Bayless brothers in their otherwise normal home, even the justifiably confused rattlesnake in a haunted room, a phantomlike impression was perceived by a phantom faculty. In each case these experimenters had a brush with the unseen.

FOUR

phantom faces

"One autumn evening some years ago I was walking home in a London street, walking briskly in the face of a strong southwest wind, the one I love best of all winds in this hemisphere, thinking of nothing except that I was thirsty for my cup of tea and that the wind was delightful when something extraordinary occurred, something never hitherto experienced. This was the appearance of a face—the face of a girl well known and very dear to me, who lived at the time at home with her people at a distance of eighty miles from where I was. It was the face only, the vivid image of the face, so vividly seen that it could not have appeared a more real human face if the girl had actually come before me. But, as I said, since it did not rest still for one instant, but had a flutter like the flutter we used to see in a cinematograph picture, and continually moved to and fro and vanished and reappeared about every second, always keeping on a level with and about three feet removed from my eyes. The flutter and motion generally was like that of a flag or of some filmy substance agitated by the wind. Then it vanished and I saw it no more."

This quotation is from the book *A Hind in Richmond Park* by the famous British naturalist and writer W. H. Hudson. This was Hudson's last book, a gentle almost Victorian piece of writing. Hudson was acutely sensitive to nature, which perhaps accounts for his sensitivity to psychic impressions as well since both reveal an aptitude for total absorption away from the self.

For some reason the wind seemed associated with his phantasmal experience. Hudson, as he stated, was especially fond of breezes and some of his psychical experiences occurred while he was preoccupied with the play of the wind about his face. This account of his first vision of a face in the wind was veridical, for the face heralded a trauma in the life of the young girl. After the vision he wrote to the girl's parents, but they reported that all was well. However, they were actually covering up a very distressing situation. The parents had been pressing the girl, then only fourteen, about declaring firm religious convictions. At the time her face was seen the girl had, in an unexpected display of revolt, threatened to run away from her family for she could no longer stand the pressure they were exerting upon her.

Hudson had another psychical experience while visiting the Cornish coast. A violent and cold wind was blowing over the coast at the time. He had gone out to bird-watch but discovered that he had left his gloves behind on some rocks where he had stopped to rest. Forgetting the bird-watching, Hudson decided to retrace his steps to retrieve his gloves: "This, simply, was the sole subject occupying my mind, when suddenly once more I had the strange experience of a face fluttering before me—just a face as on the former occasion, just as real as in appearance, at the same distance from my eyes, fluttering, moving as if blown to and fro, appearing and disappearing as before. It was the face of a lady, an intimate and dear friend who was at a distance of something under four hundred miles from me at that moment. As in the former case, I concluded that it was a telepathic message, and in that belief I rest."

Hudson's experiences are unique. The faces were always seen projected against the wind. Yet on another level his experiences are similar to many cases of phantom faces. Apparitions do not necessarily appear as full-bodied forms. In many instances only part of a figure appears. We recognize one another by certain visual features, usually the face, and many phantoms show only that portion of the human figure which may be recognized, from the bust up or just the face.

The Reverend Charles Tweedale was an English clergyman and

amateur astronomer with an avid interest in the psychic. His wife was a gifted sensitive and his vicarage was haunted. Tweedale himself was peculiarly gifted with psychic abilities and on more than one occasion saw phantom faces. The following example was sent to the publication *The English Mechanic and World of Science*.

Tweedale had gone to bed early but was awakened from his sleep for no apparent reason. He glanced about the darkened room, illuminated only by a bright, glistening moon. His eyes fastened upon the panels of a wardrobe cupboard lit up by a shaft of moonlight from the window. While he gazed at the wood panels a form suddenly appeared. "Indistinct at first, it gradually grew clearer, until I recognized the face of my grandmother. I had been observing it for some seconds, when the vision melted away gradually, and disappeared in the moonlight. An unusual thing struck me, and stamped itself upon my mind: it was the fact that my grandmother had on an old-fashioned cap, which was fluted in a shell-like design."

The next morning Tweedale related his experience to his parents. His father became very agitated and left the breakfast table, leaving his wife to explain that the night before, simultaneously to the Reverend Tweedale's experience, his father had reported a similar vision of a form by his bed. A few hours later a telegram announcing the death arrived. Not only this, but upon further inquiry it was discovered that an aunt had also seen the same figure. All three had seen the phantom at approximately the same time. Upon checking into the death, witnesses at the old woman's deathbed verified that during her final illness she had worn a shell-like cap and had it on when she died.

Others have also seen phantom faces, as the next case from the two-volume collection of psychic experiences *Phantasms of the Living* indicates. In this case the percipient saw the apparition of his infant son. "On January 24, 1881, at half past seven in the morning, I was suddenly awakened by hearing his voice, as I fancied, very near me. I saw a bright, opaque, white mass before my eyes, and in the center of this light I saw the face of my little darling, his eyes bright, his mouth smiling. This apparition, accompanied by the sound of his voice, was too short and too sudden to be called a dream, it was too clear, too decided to be called an effect of imagination. So distinctly did I hear his voice that I looked around the room to see whether he was actually there." It was later verified that the boy had died at the same time his phantom was seen.

Are these faces real in the physical sense or are they hallucinations engendered by the thoughts of the living or dead? Such a question has no easy answer. Many times these phantom faces are seen projected onto surfaces, walls, or appear as reflections. To some extent they are similar to visions seen in crystal gazing. Crystal gazing, or scrying as it is often called, is an age-old practice. No doubt everyone has seen late-night movies where the medium looks like a renegade from a gypsy camp staring into a huge glass ball to get "psychic vibrations." Nonetheless crystal gazing can lead to the uncovering of psychical impressions. The blank glass, crystal, pan of water, or whatever may be used can serve as a means for catching the scryer's attention. Finally, the subject's own mind projects visions and pictures into the glass which may actually represent projections of telepathic impressions using this momentary state of mental passivity or dissociation to break away from the unconscious into the conscious mind.

One of the most successful clairvoyants who used this technique was Mrs. A. Goodrich-Freer, who besides having psychic ability was an investigator of haunted houses and all things psychical. While visiting friends, on one occasion, she stared into a brightly polished piece of mahagony to see if she could get impressions of a picnic which some friends were planning. Soon Mrs. Goodrich-Freer saw vivid images which resolved into a grassy scene which she described in detail. She saw one member of the party with an injured back. A few days later during the picnic, which was enjoyed in a setting very like the one Mrs. Goodrich-Freer had described, one of the members did hurt her back.

In this case the visions were seen against a polished surface. This case is similar to the following, where a figure was also seen, not as an apparitional form, but as a phantom reflection on a piece of polished furniture.

Six weeks after the death of a Captain Towns in Sidney, Australia, three acquaintances of his paying their respects, were entering a room in the late Captain's house. On the surface of a wardrobe appeared the image of Captain Towns, so lifelike that all three thought it was a portrait. The Captain's daughter entered the room and also saw the figure. His widow saw the phantom reflection and ventured to move her hand over the polished surface of the cabinet. As she did so, the phantom faded away. All in all, more than five people saw the motionless figure.

Now, it might be argued that since the phantom was collectively seen, it could not be analogous to the images seen during crystal gazing. This would not be quite accurate since in some cases crystal images are seen collectively. Mrs. Goodrich-Freer once recorded that she was imagining a nicely decorated room in her crystal. The vision was being shared by a fellow scryer. Mrs. Goodrich-Freer ventured to imagine another piece of furniture into the setting which her confrere immediately recorded seeing as Goodrich-Freer began nonverbally constructing the revision. In this case the two minds had become extrasensorily en rapport. Can collectively seen phantom faces be of a similar nature?

Unlike apparitional faces and images seen during crystal gazing some phantom faces seem to be unnervingly "real," as in the following case. The sea harbors many mysteries—ghost ships, disappearing islands, strange beasts, and other enigmas. However, no mystery is as bizarre and well-evidenced as the phantom faces that haunted the S.S. *Watertown*.

The *Watertown* was a large oil tanker owned by the Cities Service Company. In December 1924 a tragic accident occurred on board the ship. Two seamen, James Courtney and Michael Meehan, were cleaning a cargo tank while the ship was en route to the Panama Canal from the Pacific Coast. Both men were overcome by gas fumes and died. In true maritime tradition they were buried at sea on December 4, 1924.

The next day the phantom faces appeared. The first mate reported to the captain, Keith Tracy, that two faces were following the ship in the water. All the crew, as well as the captain, saw the faces of the two dead men, continually appearing day after day as the ship slowly made its way to the Panama Canal. When the ship docked in New Orleans the captain reported the bizarre events to officials of the Cities Service Company and J. S. Patton, of the company, suggested that the captain try to photograph the faces. The first mate owned a camera and Patton gave a sealed roll of film to the captain, who supervised the loading of the camera, hoping to procure a photograph of the faces.

The captain's hopes were fulfilled. When the *Watertown* set sail for its return voyage the phantoms again appeared. Six photographs were taken of the heads, but the film was not developed until the ship again docked in New Orleans. The film was delivered to J. S. Patton, who sent it to a commercial developer. Five of the photographs showed nothing, but a sixth revealed two heads very distinctly projected on the water dolorously following the ship.

Two attempts have been made to follow up the *Watertown* case in the hope of obtaining more facts. The first was by Hereward Carrington, the veteran psychical investigator. It was Carrington who dug out many of the facts on the case. The incident was originally recorded in the Cities Service Company's own magazine *Service* in 1934. The account was highly inaccurate, as Carrington was able to discover. Interviews were attempted with those involved in the case but, unfortunately, Patton and the first mate had died and the captain and most of the original crew had long since dispersed and could not be located. Carrington was able to interview the manager of the company's New York office, Mr. Storey. The New York office had at one time publicly displayed a blow-up of the snapshot. The photographer who developed the film could not be traced and even more disappointing, no official report had ever been placed on file. Carrington was able to procure some interesting facts about the faces themselves. The faces appeared only occasionally, appearing and disappearing on and off, the appearances lasting only a few brief moments, and seemed stationary. They would always appear at a set distance from the vessel. The heads were always the same size, larger than life-size, and always maintained the same relationship to each other.

The other attempt at delving into the events occurring on the *Watertown* was made thirty years after the incident by Michael Mann. In 1957 *Fate* magazine ran an account of the *Watertown* case which was incomplete. No copy of the photograph could be secured. Mann was intrigued by the account and spent five years tracing the case and ultimately secured a copy of the photograph. He uncovered the fact that after the photographs were taken and sworn to by Captain Tracy and his assistant engineer, Monroe Atkins, the film was checked for fakery by the Burns Detective Agency. The negatives were returned and became the property of the owners of the ship. Mann also discovered that the photograph showed the two faces in the same position as recorded by the numerous witnesses.

There are other mysteries about the *Watertown* incident besides the faces. These faces were so clear that the entire crew saw them, yet when they were photographed only one out of six snapshots was successful in recording them. Apparently the faces were "real" enough to be collectively seen, but not always clear enough to be photographed. On the other hand, whatever force created the images was not consistent enough to support the figures for more than a few moments. The fact that they were seen always at the same place rules out the highly unlikely possibility that the faces were caused by chance configurations in the water. Ultimately, the faces died away, and with it one of the most baffling and bizarre mysteries of the sea. I know of no other case occurring at sea like it.

The fact that faces have appeared on film is not a new one. The art of photography was discovered in 1839 and by 1870 many psychics were claiming that they could photograph the faces of the dead. The phenomenon became known as spirit photography. Usually the client would pose while his picture was taken by the psychic and when the photograph was developed an extra face would appear on the print, often recognized as that of a deceased friend or relative.

The early history of spirit photography is not very impressive. The first practitioner of this art was a Boston engraver, William Mumler, who photographed himself one day and on the plate appeared a female form. Public interest was aroused and soon Mumler opened up trade as a professional spirit photographer. Unluckily, one spirit "extra" turned out to be a sitter Mumler had photographed a few weeks earlier, whose image he had exposed onto the new plate. Mumler made a hasty retreat, reappeared later in New York, got into legal difficulties there, and disappeared from the psychic scene permanently.

By this time other spirit photographers had emerged to take advantage of a good thing. One of the most famous was Frederick Hudson, whose spirit extras were soon found to be double exposures. In France, Buguet maintained a lucrative career until police uncovered all sorts of cardboard figures and other sundries which Buguet had used as props for his photographs. Despite these

The S.S. Watertown *photograph of the two faces which followed the ship.*

The spirit photograph of Flora Loudon taken by Ed Wyllie during experiments with the Reverend Charles Cook.

disclosures, though, a few spirit photographers did succeed in presenting an a priori case that the phenomenon was worthy of serious attention. Among these were William Hope and Mrs. Emma Deane. Although they were each accused of fraud at one time or another (and what psychic isn't?), several photographs taken by them were undoubtedly genuine. For example, Hope once produced a photograph of a dead figure of which no likeness had ever been taken during life. Several such oddities occur in the history of spirit photography.

Unfortunately, it is extremely difficult to investigate spirit photography because of all the possible methods of faking the results. One may imprint faces by a little device called a ghost stamp, which can be palmed in the hand and which can print a little "extra" on a photograph in an instant. Very artistic double exposures can be made. Or film already rigged with extra faces can be substituted for the original film.

However, there was one spirit photographer who seems to have escaped the stigma of fraud. Not only that, one of his phantom photographs serves as probably the most evidential spirit extra ever taken. Ed Wyllie (1848–1911) was a Californian who worked as a photographer in Los Angeles. His business became threatened when spots and odd light streaks began appearing on his photographs, ruining them. Gradually these spots turned into faces. Inadvertently Wyllie had become a spirit photographer. For several years, both in the United States and in England, Wyllie demonstrated his abilities. In 1910 the Pasadena Society for Psychical Research experimented at great length with him and ultimately supported his claims. Some of these investigations were written up in a little book, *Unseen Faces Photographed* by H. A. Reid. The Pasadena Society was basically an amateur group whose main prestige came many years later when the famous writer Upton Sinclair became active in it.

Only two incidents mar an otherwise blameless career (and this is quite something for a spirit photographer!). One critic, P. A. Jensen, accused Wyllie of imprinting his spirit extras by means of a prepared negative superimposed onto the photograph. There was no direct evidence for this accusation other than a suspicious negative found in a house where Wyllie had been. Jensen, however, could not further verify his claim. Another critic accused Wyllie of faking his spirit pictures by the use of a photograph prepared with luminous paint which was held over the photographic plates before they were exposed. The critic, Dr. Woillard, testified that Wyllie had shown him the method after being bribed to tell how photographs were faked. However, since Wyllie was a professional photographer he certainly would be well aware of how to fake psychic results as well as to procure genuine ones.

However, a few of Wyllie's photographs simply cannot be dismissed. James Coates, an English enthusiast interested in psychic photography, sent Wyllie an object and asked him to try to get a spirit extra without his being present. Wyllie sent Coates, whom he had never met, a print with an extra resembling Coates's grandmother. Coates was so impressed that he invited the Californian to England, where he set up a controlled series of tests with complete strangers to Wyllie as sitters. Results were good and 25 percent of the spirit extras achieved were recognized.

The most impressive photographs and the most systematic experiments carried out with Wyllie were those designed by the Reverend Charles Cook. The results were so extraordinary that the experiments were published in the *Journal* of the ASPR with a lengthy introduction by Dr. James Hyslop.

Evaluating cases of spirit photography is very difficult because there are so many ways it can be faked. Another problem is that human testimony is notoriously inaccurate since it is very difficult for anyone to report accurately what exactly happened at a given moment. Both psychologists and psychical researchers have carried out experiments in human observation and all the findings uniformly show that human observation and memory are so faulty that they cannot be relied upon to any great extent. In Dr. Cook's experiments this same problem arose, yet one case is striking because of the identification of the extra, a person that Wyllie could not possibly have known. Cook carefully conducted his experiments with full awareness of how spirit photographs could be faked. His controls did not seem to be tight enough, though, for he was obviously tricked by the Colorado spirit photographer Alex Martin, whose productions were blatantly fraudulent. The following case, despite any discrepancies in the report, still remains one of the best-authenticated phantom faces recorded in the generally dubious history of psychic photography.

In 1901 Cook began his series of tests with Wyllie. He bought the plates and always kept them in his possession, usually developing the photographs himself:

> In the first two successful experiments, June 25 and 26, Mr. J. H. Disler, a capable investigator and experienced photographer, assisted me. Disler and I made a most critical and thorough examination of Mr. Wyllie's camera, lens, plate-holder, background, and all accessories. Mr. Wyllie at no time came in contact with them, but stood at one side as a spectator, in the custody of special witnesses. On one plate there was the appearance of a "bright spot" or "spot of light" resembling a cube-shaped diamond, near the elbow of my right arm, emitting rays of light in lateral directions. On the other plate there was a young girl's face somewhat blurred, but plainly visible on the upper part of my vest. The forehead appeared to be under my collar, and just above it an object like a star. This plate was developed by Mr. Disler, the photographer, in company with Dr. Cook, at Mumsey's Photographic Stores, Broadway, Los Angeles, immediately after exposure. The next experiment was made on June 27, 1901, at 11 A.M. Mr. Wyllie focused the picture and capped and uncapped the lens. The plate-holder was not out of my sight a single instant. In the darkroom my observations were critical. My attention was tensely alert that nothing escaped my notice. I watched the developing process and saw coming out on the plate an object or face before the face of the sitter became visible. It became more clearly defined as the developing process was nearing completion.
>
> Returning to the gallery (studio), as Mr. Wyllie held the negative up before the window, I saw on it a face that was very distinct even more so than my own. Comparing it with that of the preceding experiment, we saw that it was the same face that had appeared upon the day before. It covered my left shoulder, extended upon my breast, and was larger and much more distinct than the first attempt with additional accompaniments, flowing and wavy hair, encircled with a halo or luminous radiance, star-shaped flower or lily in the hair just above the forehead, and symbolic representations of a cross and heart below the face.
>
> This face I recognized as that of the young lady or girl whom I first met in the month of September of the year 1866, as a student of Antioch College at Yellow Springs, Ohio. We were classmates at that institution, and passed two years of student life together. Her home was at Higginsport on the banks of the Ohio, twenty miles above my old home. She

passed into the other life about four years after the short period of our student life together, that is, in 1873. The name is Flora Loudon.

So far the case is impressive. As can be clearly seen from the photograph that accompanied Cook's report, the delineation of the "extra" is so clear that it would be hard not to have recognized it. Further, the items accompanying the face, the lily, cross, and heart, were symbols which had a very private and intimate meaning for Cook and his relationship to Flora Loudon.

Nonetheless, a critic might argue, recognition of a spirit extra is poor evidence as the chances of malobservation are so great. This argument is, I am afraid, very valid as can be seen from the history of one spirit photographer, George Moss. Moss had a lucrative career as a spirit photographer in England and gave sittings under the auspices of the British College of Psychic Science, a sort of clearing house for mediums, operated by a wealthy spiritualist, J. Hewat MacKenzie. (This organization which folded many years ago has no relation to the current College of Psychic Studies also in London.) Moss's successful career came to an abrupt end in the 1920s when his methods of faking extras were discovered. He confessed and when his earlier photographs were reexamined they all showed the telltale marks of fakery. What is so amazing and a deathblow to human testimony is that despite the fact that all of Moss's extras were bogus, a huge percentage of these fakes had been recognized by the sitters as forms of deceased relatives or friends.

Could the Flora Loudon photograph have had a smiliar questionable identification? First, it must be remembered that Cook was a critical investigator, not the typical credulous spiritualist who usually goes to spirit photographers, trying to prove survival after death. (I am not implying that *all* spiritualists are credulous, but they do seem to have more than their share.) What is needed is outside testimony, for if two witnesses identify a spirit photograph then the chances of its authenticity are that much greater. And this is exactly the case with Wyllie's photograph of Flora Loudon.

On May 7, 1905, four years after the experiments were run, Cook was lecturing on psychical research in Los Angeles. By coincidence William Loudon, Flora's uncle, happened to be visiting the city, saw a handbill of the lecture, and thought it might be an interesting diversion. Cook passed around several spirit photographs and the surprised Loudon recognized one of his niece. In a notorized statement to Cook, William Loudon wrote: "Among these pictures was one which I distinctly recognized as that of Flora Loudon, who died more than thirty years ago. Her death occurred shortly after her return from Washington, D.C. where she had been with her grandfather, General Loudon, to witness the ceremonies of the inauguration of General Grant as President of the United States. She was my niece, and during her life I was in her company very often, and knew her intimately, and hence am able to aver, from my own personal knowledge, that the aforesaid photograph bears a most striking resemblance to the original, as I knew her near the time of her decease. So far as I know, there was never taken during the life of Flora Loudon a photograph of her, with such symbols as are seen in said photography, shown me by Dr. Cook."

Since Flora had been dead for so long and had lived in an area distant from Los Angeles this evidence is striking. Many researchers downgrade the evidence for spirit photography because of its disreputable history. However, a deep investigation into this phenomenon reveals some impressive cases.

A more recent case of a highly evidential phantom face appearing during a photographic experiment concerns a remarkable psychic, Attila von Szalay. In a previous book, *The Welcoming Silence,* I reported on a short series of tests with Mr. von Szalay which attempted to tape-record "paranormal voices." In these experiments von Szalay sits while a tape recorder runs; when the tape is replayed extra voices are revealed. Often these voices call our names, etc. These experiments were run long before the current fad in tape-recording paranormal voices began when a European investigator, Konstantin Raudive, claimed to have discovered a similar effect. My original experiments were reported to the *Journal of Paraphysics* and carried on the pioneering work of Raymond Bayless which appeared in the *Journal* of the ASPR in 1959. Mr. von Szalay's talents are varied and consist of spontaneous telekinetic effects and photographic effects. On rare occasions he also has the ability to project his own image to a distant place.

The following case has been called the NAD/Kelly case and was previously reported in *Fate* magazine, *Psychic News,* and in a completely inaccurate version in a little book, *Spirit Photography,* by Tom Patterson. Luckily the chief investigator and witness, Raymond Bayless, has given me copies of the original file on this fascinating case.

On June 6, 1952 Mr. Bayless and Mr. von Szalay were at the latter's photographic studio when they were unexpectedly joined by Miss Michaela Kelly and Mrs. Gretchen Lombardo, two casual acquaintances. Mr. Bayless suggested an impromptu experiment at psychic photography with a hypnotized subject. Miss Kelly volunteered. The two men took a piece of 8'' x 10'' enlarging paper from a newly opened packet and hastily cut two pieces at random for the experiment. One piece was placed under the hands of the hypnotized subject in von Szalay's presence.

After leaving the piece of paper in that position for a while von Szalay retrieved it and plunged it into a developing tray. Obviously, under normal conditions, nothing should have appeared on that paper, yet immediately, letters began to form. These letters spelled out NAD, set against a cartoonish picture of an aged female face with a shawl dangling behind it. Later, upon being awakened and shown the print, Miss Kelly was amazed. Many years before she had had a housekeeper named Naddie, an oldish woman who always wore a shawl. The woman had been dead close to fifteen years.

Could the case have been a fake? Knowing Mr. von Szalay very well I can safely say it was not, but to the critic other factors tell against the photograph having been a deliberate fraud. The entire experiment was suggested and carried out by Raymond Bayless, who is very well acquainted with methods of photographic hanky-panky. In fact, we have jointly investigated cases of alleged psychic photography. Thus any collusion or prior arrangement would have been impossible. However, in what must have been a first for a psychic, Mr. von Szalay braved a lie-detector examination on television to prove his claims.

Now most people will claim that a lie detector can be beaten. If a person is deliberately and willfully lying this is not so. The old galvanometer lie detector was inaccurate but the polygraph used today is close to being a foolproof detector. Von Szalay appeared on a television show, *Lie Detector,* and calmly answered a number of direct questions about the NAD/Kelly photograph. He was asked pointblank if he had faked the picture or had had it faked for him. He replied that he had not. After his appearance the station management gave Mr. von Szalay a written statement to the effect that on all questions asked he had told the truth. If the reader thinks he can beat a lie detector, let him try his luck!.

Miss Kelly's own statement about the NAD photograph reads: "The undersigned, Miss Michaela Kelly, attests to the fact that the psychic astrograph received on June 6th, 1952, while held in the hand of said Michaela Kelly, produced a portrait of our housekeeper, an aged woman named NADDIE, who usually wore an old shawl about her head, said shawl apparently showing on picture. An abbreviation of her name, NAD, appears beside her portrait."

Mrs. Gretchen Lombardo witnessed the statement and also testified that the name NAD meant nothing to her nor had she known of such a woman until Miss Kelly had explained the significance.

In the *Watertown* case faces were seen, but they were hard to photograph. In the Flora Loudon and NAD/Kelly cases the faces were invisible, yet photographed with apparent ease. My final case is one where the faces were both seen and photographed—since they were completely objective.

While attending the 1972 Convention of the Parapsychological Association in Edinburgh I made the acquaintance of Dr. Hans Bender. Dr. Bender was preparing a film demonstration on "psychic surgery," a rather puerile trick in which the psychic claims to withdraw diseased organic matter from the patient through painless psychical surgery—the flesh opening up at the will of the psychic. The phenomenon had become very prevalent in South America and the Philippines. These "surgeries" are nothing more than sleight-of-hand exhibitions that for some unfathomable mystery have utterly fooled many onlookers—including some parapsychologists. Fraud is easily discernible to the critical eye. Bender was trying to expose this "phenomenon" which was the talk of Europe. Since I had had some contact with exposing this same "phenomenon" in the United States I offered Bender my background material on the fraud involved.

After this presentation Bender gave a further report on a mysterious haunting in Belméz, Spain. The case so fascinated me that I

The NAD-Kelly picture produced by Attila von Szalay working with a hypnotized subject.

One of the first faces to appear in the Belméz haunting. The part of the floor on which it appeared was cut out.

A collage of faces in the Belméz house. (COURTESY OF DR. HANS BENDER)

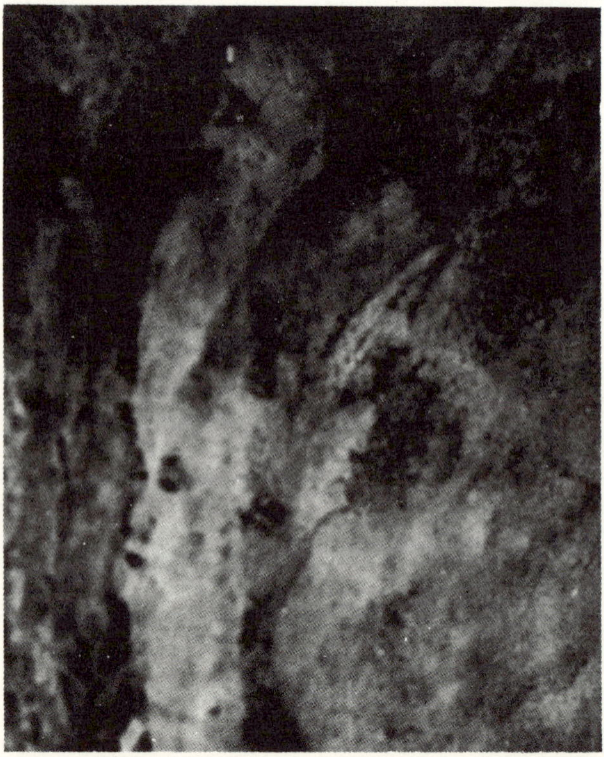

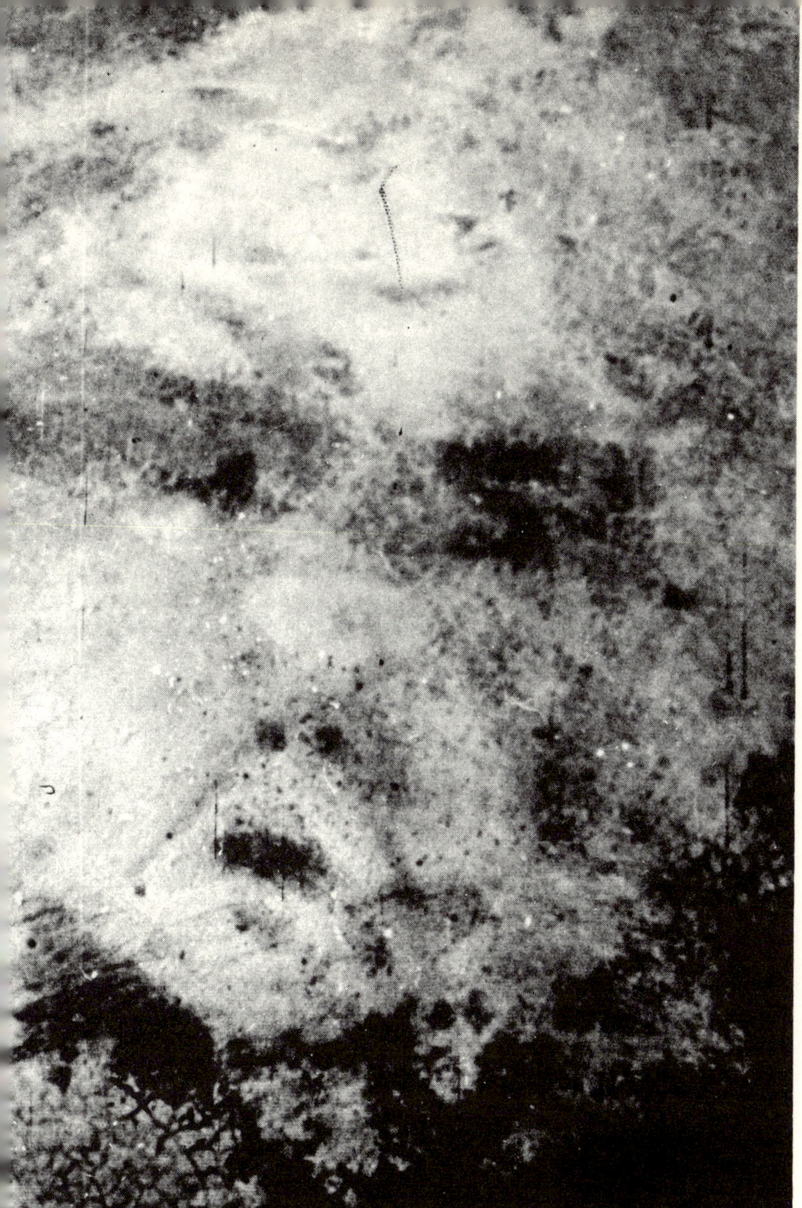

A miscellaneous face which appeared in the haunted house in Belméz on December 4, 1971. (COURTESY OF THE INSTITUTE FOR THE FRONTIERS OF PSYCHOLOGY AND PSYCHOHYGIENE, UNIVERSITY OF FREIBURG)

asked for and received further details from Dr. Bender. At present the haunting—if that is what it is—is still in action though no formal report has yet been made.

In the fall of 1971 a small concrete house in Belméz suddenly manifested an unusual phenomenon. Small faces began to appear on the floors. These faces were rather inartistic, almost caricatures, and seemed to form right out of the configurations in the concrete. The family who resided in the house became quite frightened and destroyed the first of these mysterious faces. News of the weird event flashed through Belméz and it was investigated by the alcalde, who was convinced that the faces were genuine. The house became quite a tourist attraction and the faces continued to appear. They were miniatures, a few inches around, that would gradually form and then, once formed, remain permanently in the concrete. The furore over this phenomenon caused the political and religious authorities to quarantine the house from the curious.

Hans Bender, luckily, got wind of the case and the Spanish authorities allowed him and a team of investigators to check into it. Bender is now Germany's most active researcher and has single-handedly brought parapsychology to scientific respectability there. Heading an institute in Freiburg for the study of psychical phenomena, he is an active field investigator and has authenticated several fascinating infested houses.

During his initial investigation at Belméz, Bender was not able to see the actual formation of the faces. However, he did have a sheet of light, transparent material secured over the floor in the hope that faces would still appear under it, thus ruling out painting of some sort. Faces were said to have so appeared, but Bender did not witness this himself. Time was limited and it was only after a few months that he was able to make a return visit and investigate the haunting with the Spanish parapsychologist German de Argumosa. This second investigation was in October 1972. In March 1973 Dr. Bender wrote me of his further activities, explaining that as the investigation was still going on he had not yet made his report. He also attached some notes on his second investigation which I quote: "I attached a plastic plate on the cement floor where the faces appear, as a safe-guard for fraud. This plate had to be taken off last month, as condensed water under the plate made continuous observation impossible. Faces are said to have appeared under the plate, but the photographer spoilt the photos."

There the case rests, one of the oddest curiosities in current psychical research. Since all attempts at investigation have been rather abortive so far no verdict on the Belméz faces can be made. Fortunately, Dr. Bender was able to get photographs of the earlier faces which he showed me in Edinburgh. I had suggested to him that he take scrapings from the faces to have a chemical analysis done since any sort of paint would, of course, be revealed in that way. This obvious test does not seem to have been made and there is good reason to do so since there are chemicals that can be applied to a surface which are themselves invisible, yet when sprayed with another solution, become visible. Certain treatments will result in different colors. Several of these chemicals exist for painting canvases and I am sure a similar method could be devised on concrete. The faces, then, could be rigged in advance and then brought forth at a strategic time, by quickly exposing them to another solution. Tincture of iron works very well for this!

Of course, if faces still manage to appear under a plastic plate, another explanation must be found. In psychical research discovering a mystery is only one half the game. Explaining it is the other.

FIVE

phantom voices

Scanning the entire gamut of paranormal experience, no encounter indicates the unseen presence of a human intelligence more than the sound of a disembodied voice. In my report of the haunted house in which I lived, I mentioned how, on one occasion, a hoarse, whispering voice spoke three words. There was no one in the house who could have uttered these sounds. They seemed to come out of thin air.

Paranormal voices are an extremely rare form of psychical phenomena. Nonetheless, several haunting and poltergeist cases are on record in which voices were heard. Sometimes these voices were heralded by whistling sounds which eventually consolidated into voices.

One rather violent haunting-poltergeist was the Bell Witch. The chronicle of this outbreak started in the early 1800s. The haunting began with raps and scraping sounds on the doors and windows. These sounds increased in intensity and scope until, a year later, objects began to move by themselves and stones bombarded the inside of the house. The entire history of the Bell Witch was recorded by W. V. Ingram, who took reports directly from the surviving members of the Bell family and wrote the account in his book, *An Authenticated History of the Famous Bell Witch*. Of the testimony recreated in the book, Ingram records: "The phantom continued to develop force, and visitors persisted in urging the witch [the term given the unseen intelligence behind the manifestations] to talk, and tell what was wanted, and finally it commenced whistling when spoken to, in a low, broken sound, as if trying to speak in a whistling voice." Later clearer voices were heard.

Another rather old account of a "talking" haunting is that of Willington Mill. Willington Mill was the scene of many apparitional sightings, some of human forms, some of animals. J. Proctor, who lived in the house and who kept a diary of these strange events, recorded that on occasion he would hear human whistling sounds.

In 1612 a poltergeist broke out in France centering on François Perrault, who was a key figure in the Huguenot revival. Objects were hurled about in his presence and odd noises plagued him. Finally, "In the end, . . . the wicked spirit made himself openly known for such as he was. For in the presence of us all, M. Tornus being one of the company, he began to whistle three or four times with a very loud and shrill tone, and presently to frame an articulate and intelligent voice, though somewhat hoarse, which seemed to be about three or four steps from us. . . ." *

It is generally established that a poltergeist centers on an individual. Similarly, phantom voices often focus on one person. Like voices heard in poltergeist and haunting cases, these independent voices are often fragmented, muffled, or distorted. On rarer occasions they manifest more clearly.

One of the most interesting investigations of phantom voices is the puzzling case of Mrs. Elizabeth Blake, an elderly crippled woman living in Ohio whose phantom voices convinced many an investigator. The case came to the attention of David Abbott, a magician, whose main claim to fame was a scathing book he had written, *Behind the Scenes with the Mediums,* a lengthy exposé of how mediums fake their results. Abbott was introduced to the case through a letter he received from another magician, E. A. Parsons. Parsons had investigated Mrs. Blake and was astounded by what he had witnessed. When he called to see Mrs. Blake he had found her confined to a chair with two speaking trumpets beside her. She

* A. R. G. Owen in his *Can We Explain the Poltergeist?* offers a number of other cases of voices heard during poltergeist outbreaks.

hooked these two metal trumpets together at their large, open ends thus producing a makeshift submarine-shaped trumpet. In full light phantom whispers would be heard produced within the apparatus. Mrs. Blake would sit silently during the entire sitting. Parsons himself not only heard these voices but had received information that the medium could not have normally known. As he wrote in his letter to Abbott, "During this time the lady's mouth and lips are tightly closed and she makes no motions of the throat or lips. She will, instead of holding the trumpet to her ear, hold her palm against it; or allow him to place one end of it against her back. She will, if preferred, permit two spectators to each hold an end, she merely touching the center with her fingers. In either event one hears the whispering just the same. Now this is done in broad daylight even out of doors. I investigated this phenomenon seven hours altogether, giving it every possible test, but could obtain no clue to it."

On investigating these claims further Abbott discovered that Parsons was actually a famous magician of the day whose stage name was Henry Hardin. Because Hardin was well-known in magic circles Abbott felt that the testimony of this accomplished conjurer forced him into investigating the case for himself in the hopes of either exposing a particularly ingenious fraud or witnessing a genuine phenomenon—something for which Abbott had searched for years.

Abbott secured the services of James Hyslop of the ASPR and his own cousin and fellow skeptic, George Clawson. The three met in Ohio to test Mrs. Blake. Arriving first at the Blake home, Abbott and Clawson found the elderly but congenial woman sitting in her chair. She explained that her age and illness had considerably weakened her phenomenon. However, Clawson seated himself by the medium and lifted up the trumpet by one end as Mrs. Blake placed her palm over her end of the device. At that time Abbott himself heard a tiny voice emanate from the trumpet: "I thought I heard a faint whisper in the end of the trumpet that Mr. Clawson was holding. It was however faint, so faint that I could not be certain of it. It was more like a single syllable. . . ."

Clawson lifted the trumpet to his ear. Abbott heard the whispers while Mrs. Blake was under his surveillance, but he could not understand what was said. Clawson could not decipher the muffled but multitudinous whispers either and turned the trumpet over to Abbott.

The voices were still unintelligible although Abbott could definitely ascertain that they were human voices. Finally, a quick sentence was spoken: "I am your brother and I want to talk to mother. Tell her . . . [voice became unclear]." A child's voice then made an abortive attempt to communicate. A little later a voice blurted out, "I want to talk to my brother Davie—brother Davie Abbott." This was a startling sentence since Abbott and his colleague had come to Mrs. Blake anonymously.

Clawson again took up the trumpet. He was very interested in trying to get some sort of communication from his recently deceased daughter, Georgia, and Abbott had brought him along in the hope that the recent tragedy might serve as a good test if Georgia's name were spoken by the voices. He was not disappointed. A tiny voice spoke through the trumpet saying that her mother was called "Muz" and sometimes "Muzzie." This was correct since Georgia had used these pet names for her mother. Abbott once again took over control of the trumpet and heard several voices, some of which repeated names of his deceased relatives.

Later that day Clawson and Abbott returned to the Blake residence, this time with Hyslop, who had just arrived from the East Coast to join them. Several more voices spoke through the trumpet and offered names which Abbott and Clawson recognized as being those of relatives and friends who had died. Finally a voice spoke to Abbott offering the name Harvey. Abbott had an uncle, David Harvey, who had died. The voice especially astounded Abbott, who wrote concerning his impression: "One remarkable feature of the voice which claimed to be that of my uncle David was that it resembled his voice when alive, to an extent *sufficient to call to my mind a mental picture of his appearance;* and for an instant to give me that inner feeling of his presence that hearing a well-known voice always produces in one. *I said nothing of this at the time.* I may say that during all of our sittings, no other voice bore any resemblance to the voice of the person to whom it claimed to belong, so far as I was able to detect. As this uncle had died only a few years before, I have a vivid remembrance of his voice."

After the sitting Clawson remarked spontaneously on the uncanny resemblance of the "David Harvey" voice to that of his dead relative's voice as he remembered it.

The following day more tests were carried out. Similar evidential results were secured, including a voice offering the name Georgia, as Clawson and Abbott had hoped. The voice also correctly gave the name of the city in which she had lived and the nickname of her boyfriend, Archimedes.

Abbott requested that Mrs. Blake journey into town in order to have a picture taken with Hyslop, Clawson, and himself. The journey and excitement stimulated Mrs. Blake and in the photographic studio more voices broke out from the metal trumpet. The voices were much louder, and again proper names and identifications were given.

Abbott went away puzzled by the entire affair. Although readily convinced that the knowledge the voices communicated was paranormally acquired, he could not overcome his magician's bias in order to accept that the voices were actually independent of Mrs. Blake. Ultimately, Abbott proffered the improbable theory that perhaps by some odd physiological quirk Mrs. Blake could speak through her ears. Hyslop, in conjunction with his assistant, Hereward Carrington, attempted to see if they could reproduce Mrs. Blake's effects normally, but their experiments showed nothing conclusive either way.

During the experiments with Mrs. Blake she was under close scrutiny and never moved her lips while both masculine and feminine voices were produced. Abbott did claim that he saw Mrs. Blake moving her throat muscles but this did not necessarily have any connection with the production of the voices, some of which were extremely loud.

The subject of paranormal voices had its innings only recently with the experiments undertaken by Friedrich Jurgenson and Konstantin Raudive. These experiments were predated by those of Attila von Szalay and Raymond Bayless, who were the first discoverers of what has come to be known as "tape-recorded voices."

Jurgenson began his work in Sweden in 1959 after an accidental discovery. While playing his radio, it seemed as if extra voices would dart in and out of the transmitted voices. Jurgenson was perplexed by this strange development and called a friend, Arne

Weise, director of the Swedish State Television, to stop by and investigate. Weise, his wife, and Jurgenson talked a bit while a recorder taped their conversation. On playing back the tape, extra voices were discovered on it. Jurgenson also found extra voices on the tapes he had made of the bird songs he was recording in his backyard. As Arne reported, "The voice spoke in German and was very weak. I became quite chilled and my wife was frightened. There was no explanation. The whole thing was too fantastic."

These voices continued to be recorded and Jurgenson found that he could recognize several of them as belonging to deceased relatives. As with many avant-garde discoveries in psychical research, parapsychologists were the last to jump at the opportunity to investigate Jurgenson. To date only two internationally known researchers have worked with him. The first was W. G. Roll.

Roll heard about Jurgenson from Hans Bender and visited him in July 1964. During an initial informal experiment a tape machine was set up and let run as they spoke casually. On replaying the tape some odd effects were found, and a male voice spoke the Swedish word "berätta" (tell). The voice was distinct and clearly unrelated to anything spoken during the conversation. Several other isolated words and phrases were also uttered. The next day Roll improvised an experiment using separate microphones and tape machines. The experiment was partially successful. A clear voice was imprinted on the tape uttering a few words over Jurgenson's voice speaking at the same time.

Since there were innumerable technical problems in using tape machines and the voices were rather faint, Roll could come to no conclusion about the case. Hans Bender, however, has spent considerably more time with Jurgenson and in his German publications on the case has supported the genuineness of the voices.

It was not until the arrival of Konstantin Raudive on the scene that a real controversy over the tape-recorded voices broke out. Raudive is a Latvian scholar now living in Germany who was fascinated by psychical research and particularly by Jurgenson's voices. Going to Sweden, he spent considerable time co-experimenting with him.

It has long been part of psychic tradition that if one were constantly to associate with a psychic, his ability would rub off and one would himself become psychic. There is some evidence for this. For example, the great medium Gladys Osborne Leonard discovered her psychic talents while experimenting with two friends at table tilting. Later one of these friends, Blanche Cooper, became a famous psychic herself. Several other examples could be cited. This also seems to be the case with tape-recorded voices since many people who work in conjunction with those who are able to receive voices have often developed the ability themselves.

Raudive returned to Germany and began his own experiments. At first, he could hear nothing on his tapes; however, faint voices gradually started to appear. Unfortunately, these voices are often unintelligible and Raudive has frequently given them rather odd interpretations—often based on his explication that the voices use a mixture of several languages. Unfortunately, also, Raudive's method of experimentation is not at all rigorous. He puts on a tape and engages in free conversation with others. Later on the tape is played back and Raudive picks out what he feels to be paranormal voices among the various conversing voices.

Raudive published his work in a book with the English title *Breakthrough*. Before issuing the book, though, the English publisher brought Raudive to England to run a few controlled experiments. The results were not exceptional, but some voices were found on the tapes under stricter conditions than Raudive himself had previously employed.

The publication of the book caused a near riot in parapsychology. The basic attitude was reactionary. Several parapsychologists argued that Raudive was merely picking up radio interference. Others denied that "taped voices" could even exist and complained that Raudive was projecting his own ideas as to what the random sounds on the tapes meant.

These arguments are hackneyed and easily refuted. While it must be admitted that the voices are often unintelligible, very often they will call Raudive's name quite clearly. When I listened to examples of Raudive's tapes, in a few instances very clear voices were heard, even overlapping with his. It is inconceivable that radio pickups could consistently call Raudive's name or that radio pickups would consistently be picked up on Raudive's tapes, not only in Germany but in England as well.

A New York editor, Joel Honig, went to Germany to meet with Raudive and upon his return to the United States he began his own experiments. As with Raudive, at first nothing was received, but later Honig claimed to have received voices on the tapes. Honig has not, unfortunately, kept detailed records of his experiments. I visited him in the summer of 1973 in New York and he played for me one short tape he had made. The tape had been left running while he and some friends, including the New York psychic Ingo Swann, casually talked for about ten minutes. Now this type of experimentation is very inexact since despite the claims of the experimenter, it is manifestly impossible for a single person to be able to remember in a ten-minute period all that was said by a group of people. Because of this, it is hard to isolate what voice is really "extra," if any are at all. However, there was one striking voice on Honig's tape which was hard to explain away. During the discussion a piping female voice, very unlike any of the voices of those present, spoke *over* the conversation the name Ingo Swann. It would be extremely odd for someone to just recite a name like this in the middle of a casual conversation. The effect was very puzzling.

Since the publicity gained by Raudive many persons have been on the lookout for strange voices and effects on their tapes. As might be expected the great majority of people claiming to get voices are misinterpreting various coughs, chair squeakings, and other extraneous sounds. However, a few valid cases are cropping up and are of extreme interest.

One such spontaneous case was procured by a woman who was having a sitting with the well-known British psychic David Young. The woman was taping the sitting by placing the microphone and tape recorder some distance from Young and herself. Upon replaying the tape she found an extra voice and ultimately gave a copy of the tape to David Ellis. Ellis is a young chemist who, under a grant from Cambridge University given yearly for work in parapsychology, was studying Raudive and related tape-recorded voices. The tape is rather remarkable. I first heard it in the summer of 1972 when we stopped to visit Alan Gauld, one of England's top parapsychologists, while driving with Ellis from London to Edinburgh.

During our visit Ellis brought out some tapes of voices from his collection, and the Young tape was among them. We all expected to hear the usual mumbled sounds which often pass for voices but we were really in for a surprise. At first we could hear Young giving a reading to his sitter. Both voices were quite clear and obviously at some distance from the microphone. Suddenly a third voice, very gruff and masculine, clearly said, "I love you." Young had been giving impressions to his sitter allegedly from her deceased husband. Immediately after this voice spoke, and spoke directly into the microphone, Young's voice could be heard saying, "He is telling me that he loves you." When I heard the voice I immediately got the meaning of the words but said nothing. When Mrs. Gauld heard it she looked at her husband and me and said, "The voice said, 'I love you.' " This same voice appeared later on in the tape saying the same thing. The fact that there was no one in the room except the sitter and Young, plus the correlation between what the "voice" said and what Young said about his psychic impression, is staggering evidence of the voice's paranormality. Luckily this voice was so clear that misinterpretation was impossible.

My own specific interest in the area of tape-recorded voices stems from my work with Attila von Szalay. As stated before, it was really von Szalay and Raymond Bayless who discovered the effect in 1956, three years before Jurgenson rediscovered it. Although von Szalay is a gifted psychic, the study of the "voices" began as a joint research project by the two men. Both von Szalay and Bayless had long studied the mediumship of the California medium Sophie Williams. Mrs. Williams had become famous through a book, *The Mystery of the Buried Crosses,* by the noted American writer-turned-psychical researcher Hamlin Garland, who claimed to have located several Indian artifacts through Mrs. Williams's mediumship.

One of Mrs. William's phenomena was an "independent voice" similar to Mrs. Blake's. Both von Szalay and Bayless were interested to see if they could establish that Mrs. Williams's voice was really physically independent of her organism. While she was definitely able to display exceptional ESP ability, the researchers were also pretty well able to demonstrate that the "voice" was really deliberately ventriloquized—added by Mrs. Williams for stage effect.

However, their psychic odyssey did not stop there. Even though the work with Sophie Williams had failed to demonstrate the existence of an independent voice, von Szalay and Bayless started on a long series of experiments to determine if they could develop such a voice with von Szalay, who had had a long history of psychic ability. The key to these experiments, in which I was to take part some years later, was to isolate von Szalay physically from the source of the voices. Three years later, in 1959, Bayless published his first progress report on the work.

The two men set up a research headquarters in a rented room in Hollywood, California. A clothes closet was converted into an experimental chamber in which was placed a metal speaking trumpet to amplify any sounds which would occur there with a microphone placed in its mouth. A cable extended from the microphone into an amplifier and tape machine in the living room. The closet was soundproof. Sometimes a loudspeaker was also hooked up to the apparatus so that those in the living room could simultaneously hear what was occurring in the cabinet. For these experiments Bayless alone handled the tape machine, brought the tapes, and so on.

The first results came on December 5, 1956. Bayless wrote: "Mr. von Szalay, for the purposes of this particular experiment, sat in the cabinet alone for fifteen minutes. Believing that nothing was forthcoming, he left the cabinet. We then played back the tape recording expecting to hear nothing, but were surprised to hear a distinct voice say, 'This is G.' At this time I was sitting on the outside of the cabinet listening to the highly amplified loudspeaker and heard absolutely nothing."

Later during that same experiment Bayless decided to test the amplifying system. He asked von Szalay, now outside, to produce short whistles at regular intervals. Testing the apparatus, Bayless soon discovered that when von Szalay whistled, "something" from the closet whistled back over the speaker. Something was whistling into the microphone. Finally, with Bayless and von Szalay in full view of each other, double whistles were clearly heard coming from the cabinet.

In order to further isolate von Szalay from the focus of the voices, Bayless designed the following experiment: "We obtained a large upright cardboard box 15″ x 4½′ long which we placed in the center of the room. Within this 'box-cabinet' we suspended the trumpet previously used, with a microphone placed in one end and leading into the tape recorder. Mr. von Szalay and I sat in chairs one yard from the cabinet which was completely closed. . . . During this test, three human voices were recorded spaced throughout the twenty minutes that the experiment lasted. The words that were recorded were unintelligible but nevertheless the voices were definitely human."

Often the voices recorded would be frivolous and amusing as in the following example: "During an experiment on July 7, 1957, we placed the upright cardboard 'box-cabinet,' previously described, inside the closet cabinet, closed the cabinet door and remained outside the main room for 45 minutes. One clear human whisper was recorded. We then placed the box-cabinet just outside the closet-cabinet. Mr. von Szalay sat inside the box and I sat with my head positioned within it. While sitting, we heard a very feeble high-pitched whistling sound."

Later, after Bayless had left, von Szalay continued to sit and recorded a perfectly clear female voice which said, "Hot dog, Art," and then gave a twittering laugh. As Bayless notes, "Needless to say, we can offer no explanation for these strange words."

Several more experiments were run in which both Bayless and von Szalay sat outside the cabinet. Often the tapes when replayed would be imprinted with words such as "Hello" or the names of the experimenters. Some profanity was also recorded.

This is how the experiments went until 1959. By that time hundreds of voices had been recorded. Sometimes the voices would answer specific questions. Once Bayless asked aloud where his brother was. On replaying the tape both von Szalay and Bayless clearly heard the word "Bridgeport." This, in fact, was found to be so when a few days later Bayless received a letter from his brother from Bridgeport, Connecticut.

I first became interested in von Szalay after meeting Bayless in 1967. Unfortunately my arrival on the scene was a bit inopportune. Because of a health problem Bayless had ceased working with von Szalay some years before and had not even seen him for several years. When I finally tracked von Szalay down I found that he had just gone through a traumatic personal experience and his abilities had considerably waned. Nonetheless, I did run some tests with him which were successful even though the results were not as striking as his earlier ones. After a few informal and preliminary trials I ran a controlled sitting on October 26, 1968 and another controlled test on November 1.

The first sitting began at 7:00 P.M. It was held at von Szalay's photography studio and we used his darkroom, illuminated by a bright red light, as an experimental area. I had brought my own tape machine and tapes. I set up the recorder in the darkroom and placed a tape in the machine. A microphone was attached to the recorder and was placed at the mouth of the trumpet. The trumpet was half submerged in water to amplify any sound currents caused by a "voice." Von Szalay and I sat inside the darkroom. The recorder was between us; the trumpet was a foot from me on a counter; von Szalay was about five feet from it in a chair facing me. He wore headphones connected to the recording unit.

About fifteen minutes after we had begun the sitting I happened to turn my head toward the trumpet and I definitely heard a small, airy yet distinct whistle emerge from the trumpet. I called this to von Szalay's attention. He had thought that I had accidently produced the sound. We played back the tape immediately and found that the whistle had been recorded.

We sat for another hour with no results. Getting impatient, von Szalay proceeded to ask the "voices" questions in the hope that when we replayed the tape, answers would be forthcoming. We replayed the tape at fifteen-minute intervals. I should note that during these time periods von Szalay and I remained completely silent. If either of us accidentally made a noise we would immediately "call it" so that when we replayed the tape these random noises would be identified and not misinterpreted as voices. On those occasions when either von Szalay or I did speak it was very short and obviously identifiable.

We had no results until 9:00 when von Szalay asked the "voice" who would be elected President of the United States in the forthcoming election. When we replayed the tape an extremely faint voice responded, "Humphrey." This was to be proved wrong even though it was completely apropos to the question. There seems little possibility of a misinterpretation, for when we heard the voice in the playback von Szalay and I shot a glance at each other—we had both heard the voice and what it said.

At this point von Szalay and I discontinued sitting, as I suggested we stop, go out for a bite to eat, and then continue later. We left the tape recorder in its original place, went to a neighboring restaurant, and returned at 10:00 P.M. to continue the sitting.

For the next segment we left the trumpet and microphone in the cabinet-darkroom but placed the tape recorder outside it. Von Szalay and I sat outside the darkroom by the recorder. At this point someone shouted from the street outside. We quickly replayed the tape and found that the sound had not been picked up on the tape and this assured us that any voices we heard on the tape could not be due to street sounds which had escaped our notice. At about 10:50 we replayed a ten-minute section of tape. We had had no results so far and both of us vowed that this final segment would be our last for the evening. On replaying the tape we discovered a voice saying, "Hi-ya, Art," as though shouted from a long distance away.

For our second controlled test I began setting up the recorder in the darkroom as before. We sat in the reception room, twenty-five feet away. After forty-five minutes we had achieved no results. We then sat in the darkroom, as we had before. Again, as I sat, I suddenly heard a gurgle from the trumpet, which was not in water this time. Von Szalay apparently heard it through the earphones as we instantaneously shot a glance at each other. We immediately replayed the tape and found that a two-syllable word had been uttered, but it was too muffled to be understood. We achieved no other results during the rest of our experiment.

Although our tests were much less notable than the early experiments we did show some inexplicable results. After my early experiments circumstances improved for us. Raymond Bayless rejoined us and took charge of the experiments. Von Szalay's personal problems had been resolved, and finally the interest sparked by Raudive's work helped motivate von Szalay to such an extent that his results today greatly surpass his earlier results. Von Szalay now uses only a microphone and tape machine. The voices are clearer and are able to speak for a longer period of time, sometimes in lengthier sentences. Even a greater variety of voices has been recorded—male, female, and even children's voices. They have also become more consistent which helps in designing the experiments.

Raymond Bayless carried out a controlled test in the summer of 1973. Von Szalay, in full light, sat at one end of a couch while Bayless, who brought along his own portable cassette machine, sat at the other end setting the microphone with the machine on his far side. While they were sitting in this manner a clear voice, speaking a two-syllable word, was recorded.

Bayless has also recently resolved a controversial issue concerning tape-recorded voices. Some investigators feel that the voices are not physical voices picked up by the microphone but are directly impressed onto the tape via psychokinesis (PK). This would be similar to psychic photography, where a picture is projected directly onto the film. In this case though, voices are imprinted directly on the tape and the microphone has nothing to do with the voices. This explains why in the cases of the Raudive and Jurgenson tapes voices are never heard by the participants but found only on the tapes. This explanation cannot however account for the von Szalay results. While many voices are heard only after the tape is replayed, some of his voices on rare occasions can be heard independently, as witnessed during my own tests.

In order to resolve further this issue Bayless undertook a series of tests with von Szalay in which some of the experiments were made with the microphone open and some with it sealed shut to preclude its picking up any sounds at all. Voices have been recorded only when the microphone is unobstructed. Thus, it seems likely that the tape-recorded voices are in fact acoustical, and although they are usually inaudible to the human ear, are actually being produced in physical space and picked up by the microphone.

There are two possible ways of approaching the phenomenon of tape-recorded voices. One approach is that the voices are a form of mediumship and that the production of them depends on the presence of a psychic. However, Raudive has argued that he is no medium and that anyone can record voices if he has patience. He believes that he has demonstrated a form of electronic communication with the dead unhampered by the necessity of requiring the services of a medium. In support of this he argues that if he leaves the room voices can still be recorded and that many of his associates are now receiving similar results.

I prefer the first interpretation. All paranormal phenomena seem to need a catalyzing human agent. Even hauntings will skip certain tenants, which would indicate that the production of ghostly phenomena is dependent on a human psyche that can catalyze them. This also explains why in some hauntings certain residents may never witness anything paranormal while the rest of the occupants will. This "linger effect" explains why voices might still be heard when Raudive makes a temporary exit. It can also explain why so many can record voices. Raudive gained his ability after his work with Jurgenson. Likewise, Honig picked up his ability after associating with Raudive.

With von Szalay we have a similar cycle. After years of work with him, it was Bayless who systematically began to experiment to see if he could achieve results without von Szalay's presence. Sitting with his wife, he has regularly tried to tape-record voices. While results have been inconsistent, a few voices have been picked up on the tape. Since Bayless experiments alone with his wife, it is easy to pick out which extraneous voices are on the tapes. The few I have heard are quite clear.

One individual who has delved more deeply into personal experimentation with voices is William Welch, a California writer. Welch was intrigued with the whole area of tape-recorded voices and made the acquaintance of von Szalay. He was impressed by the results he witnessed and then proceeded to try his own luck. Slowly but surely voices did appear on his tapes. Some of them offered recognizable names of deceased friends and some spoke in foreign languages. Again, the tapes I have heard have been impressive.

As for myself? I am afraid that my own experiments along these lines have been generally void. I had never seriously thought about sitting for voices myself until one morning in July 1972. I awoke early in the morning and for some reason had a compulsion to drag out my cassette machine to try to record a voice. I sat at my desk and placed the recorder by my side with its little microphone before me placed in a tumbler turned on its side to make a tiny cabinet. All the while I did not really think that I would record anything.

I started the recording by verbally asking that any presence make itself known. I played back the tape every five minutes. After fifteen minutes I played the tape back routinely to listen to another segment when to my amazement a distinct male voice said the name Hitler. Oddly, this is the same name that Jurgenson recorded prolifically during his early experiments. Raudive claims to have recorded cries of "Hitler" very frequently. When Raudive's work became publicized the same name started cropping up on von Szalay's tapes, and there it was on mine. I immediately phoned Raymond Bayless to play the tape for him and he could also clearly hear the voice.

Spurred on by this success I continued all that day to experiment. I recorded absolutely nothing. The next two days were similarly engaged in recording. And I achieved the same result—nothing, absolutely nothing. To this day I have never been able to pick up another taped voice. And so my beginner's luck will have to remain merely a spontaneous oddity so typical of the way psychical phenomena seem to function.

SIX

fiery phantoms

It was when her mother was ill that Kate Christie first saw the apparition she describes as "the man of fire." The novelist was an adolescent at the time but had already been introduced to the world of phantoms through her own experiences and the psychic perceptions of her mother. The burning phantom appeared one lazy April evening as the girl lay on her bed:

"He stood between my bed and the wall; he appeared to be made of a luminous, burning substance. His hair was red, like little upright tongues of fire. On his face was a smile, not of pleasure, but like the grin of a skull. He filled me with terror." With this description Miss Christie begins a chronology of her experiences with her man of fire in her autobiographical sketch *Apparitions*. Like many phantoms which have been recorded through time, this phantom did not speak, was not recognized, nor did he ever reveal his purpose for appearing. Yet his appearances did have special meaning for Miss Christie.

Several days later the writer had a letter from her father saying that her mother had undergone an operation. What her father did not tell his vacationing daughter was that this operation was the beginning of the end. An inoperable cancer had been found. Even though the connection was vague, Kate Christie soon realized that the fiery phantom was a harbinger of dread and of death.

Before the death of her father the apparition appeared once more.

Miss Christie does not write what she saw but only what she felt. To her the apparition became an obsession. Did the apparition, with its "grin like a skull," appear, as in the old paintings of Death personified, to announce the death of a friend or relative? After his second visitation, Miss Christie's father died of a sudden stroke in front of his horrified family.

Miss Christie saw her man of fire once more, several years later. This time the apparition appeared during a period of self-questioning to which the creative mind is so often prone. According to some schools of psychology, life is a search for meaning. Taking leads from the philosophical insights of men such as Kierkegaard and Heidegger, existential psychologists believe that life must have meaning or an individual will soon be beset by depression and neuroses generated by a mind that has not found itself. Without goals there is no motivation, without motivation one is submerged and caught in an existential vacuum. It was in just such a vacuum that Miss Christie found herself during her struggles as a writer. As she questioned herself and her goals, withdrawn from interpersonal relationships and alone with her work, the phantom appeared: "He appeared one evening when I was sitting reading by the fire with all the lights on. He came in and stood beside me: the Other One, the sun-god, the burning creature with a face of classic male beauty stretched in an archaic smile, the man came in to petrify me, I was rigid in my chair, my mouth open in a silent shriek."

In this case the appearance of the phantom broke the vacuum: "I had got myself into some very deep waters—had I also got myself out of them? Had I evoked or conjured him? From where? He said nothing, did nothing, he stood there with his terrifying smile. I have never seen him since."

As with C. G. Jung, Kate Christie's experiences divided her thoughts. She could not determine whether the apparition was a projection from her own mind or an entity independent of it. This enigma exists for the reader of Miss Christie's book also. Can phantoms be projected from the mind? There is no reason that the mind cannot create thoughts that no longer restrict themselves to the provinces of the mind. Telepathy indicates that thought may become independent of the thinker. Neither can we legitimately say that thoughts are present only within the brain.

The materialist will argue that our thoughts and consciousness are only an epi-phenomenon of our organism. Just as the body has certain physiological functions that lead to the creation and secretion of such products as sweat, blood, and waste, so our brain with its elaborate mechanics secretes consciousness. Yet, despite this "common sense" argument, the mind has shown that it can appear independent not only of our brain, but of our body as well. Even more astounding, the human consciousness can even appear to be spatially separated from our organism. This is dramatically brought to the fore during the out-of-the-body experience.

So far all the people chronicled in this book have described experiences of phantoms external to themselves, either by seeing or sensing them. However, a large group of individuals have had the experience of being a phantom. That is, such individuals find that their consciousness leaves the confines of the physical body and acts independently of it. Often the percipient sees himself clothed in a phantom body closely resembling the physical body. During the experience some percipients have been known to appear to friends as apparitions of the living.

Captain Burton was a British soldier. Suffering from the effects of a heart attack he suddenly found himself a phantom. In the hospital Burton found himself "standing at the foot of my bed, looking at myself. Then suddenly I found myself dragged violently over the bed-rail where I floated above myself; following which came a tremendous crack. Then I heard the doctor's voice: 'He is coming round.' He had considered me dead for some time."

Fine, the skeptic will respond; mental patients often have weird distortions of themselves, their minds, and their bodies. Yet we do not felicitously proclaim these disturbances to be psychic phenomena. This point is well taken, but what if the out-of-the-body consciousness observes a spatially distant happening which, in fact, actually occurred? Many persons, during the out-of-the-body state, report how they "traveled" and observed the actions of other people, only to verify this exact information upon "reentering" the physical organism.

Mrs. Gladys Osborne Leonard, the famous psychic, had several verifiable out-of-the-body experiences, or "astral projections." On one occasion as she was lying on her bed she suddenly found herself leaving her physical body and in a new apparitional body. She heard her husband go to the door and an idea for an experiment struck the nimble mind of the psychic. She would go, in her new body, to see who her husband was meeting at the door. Instantly she found herself at her husband's side, invisible, and watched him take a coin out of his pocket and hand it to the visitor. Later on, in her physical body once again, she questioned her husband about the incident. It had occurred. While Mrs. Leonard was "asleep" her husband had gone to the door and given a tip to the caller, for a favor rendered.

Cases such as these radically alter how we normally think about the subjectivity and privacy of our thoughts. From the anecdotal and experimental evidence of ESP we know that thoughts and emotions, which we ordinarily view as totally subjective and nonmaterial entities, can be tapped by another mind. Perhaps our thoughts may also break away from the world of the mental and enter the world of the physical. If our mind can reach beyond the limits of the body, it may well break into the world of objective existence.

Apparitions seem trapped in this eerie world between the physical and the nonphysical. Their very traits reveal this. For example, apparitions may be collectively seen. The Morton ghost was seen by all who were present on some occasions and, in the first chapter, both Miss Verity and her sister saw the apparition of S. H. Beard. Apparitions have also been seen in mirrors, indicating the ability to cast a reflection.

The Misses Du Cane both saw an apparition that was reflected first in a mirror before it was actually seen. In this case the phantom, like Kate Christie's man of fire, glowed: "There was no light beyond that which glimmered through the venetian blinds . . . I was awe struck by the sudden appearance of a figure gliding noiselessly toward me from the outer room." The wraith was that of a young moustached man: "The face was slightly luminous, which enabled us to distinguish the features distinctly—the apparition glided towards my sisters, who were standing inside the room—and who had first caught sight of it reflected in the mirror. . . ."

So, it seems, apparitions are physical. Perhaps—but just as inexplicable are cases where apparitions, which appear to be physical entities, show characteristics of also being immaterial. The Morton ghost, remember, glided through strings placed across a staircase without disturbing them. The Du Cane apparition vanished into thin air in front of all the witnesses. Physical objects cannot do this.

Apparitions tend to be partially physical and partially immaterial. Some phantoms have moved physical objects while others are invisible to only but one percipient. Other phantoms share all these traits. Perhaps our thoughts might, under just the right conditions, flee from the id into a mode of existence just the other side of our physical world, perhaps in some form of "psychic ether."

In this respect there is really no paradox in the experiences of Jung and Miss Christie. Even though the phantoms sensed and heard by Jung and seen by Miss Christie probably were projections or thoughts from their own minds and conscious (or unconscious), they may well have been independent also. In the world of the psychical, "thoughts may become things." Like the world of Alice in Wonderland, everything is topsy-turvey.

It is here that a precept from Buddhist thought becomes pertinent. According to some Mahayana Buddhist thought the reason we cannot directly perceive and understand the universe is that we think categorically in terms of the objective and the subjective. In Buddhist thought this is decried as a fallacy, for there is no difference between the perceived and the perceiver. Both are just manifestations of the same great unifying void.

The characteristics of apparitions, out-of-the-body experiences, and even mystical experiences indicate that this Buddhist doctrine has some validity. It is also tempting to reason that, possibly, psychical phenomena are so enigmatic and confusing to us not because the phenomena themselves are so bizarre but because our Western concept of thinking and of viewing the world is based on so many mistakes and misconceptions that we could not hope to understand them.

Again, Eastern thought has labeled all our "perceptions" as illusion. Perhaps this is truly the case. In recent years many parapsychologists have discovered an intellectual and practical challenge in the study of Eastern religions, cultures, and their attitude toward the paranormal. This may suggest that only if we alter our entire way of thinking might the psychic become comprehensible.

Miss Christie dubbed her phantom the "man of fire" because he seemed to be glowing and burning. The apparition that the Du Cane sisters saw also gleamed in a dark room. Just why apparitions glow and on occasion even become fiery is a question to be left for later. However, reports of phantoms from the Victorian age, as well as reports gathered just recently, comment on the luminescence of apparitions. This trait was also reported centuries ago in cases of phantoms recorded in religious writings. These apparitions were once thought to come from the cleansing and flaming world of purgatory. All these specters share certain similarities.

Shining apparitions were especially represented in those cases collected by the Society for Psychical Research. In the following case the Reverend W. G. Grignol collected the testimony of Mr. and Mrs. Davis, investigated the case, and submitted it to the Society for Psychical Research.

Mrs. Davis was the first to see the figure. "I fell asleep at once but was awakened by an unusual light in my room. I sprang up in a tremor exclaiming, 'What is it?' and saw gliding by my bed the figure of an elderly person which went through the closed door leading into Mr. Davis's room."

Mr. Davis also reported: "I was awakened from a quiet sleep by a light which seemed to come in at the door leading from my wife's chamber, and immediately a figure appeared, approached my bed and leaned over as if to kiss me—then suddenly passed away, but not before I had recognized in the features of the apparition those of my mother, who died in 1872 aged 81."

Frederic Myers also contributed a phantasmal experience in which radiant light accompanied the phantom. The percipient's name was not revealed. This is not odd. While talking of one's psychical experience has now become much in vogue, the Victorians lived in a world of restraint. Reports of such experiences were a social taboo and the close of the Victorian age was permeated with an atmosphere filled with such an enthusiasm for science and logic that to admit to psychic experiences would not only be frowned upon but likely to be diagnosed as a product of mental imbalance. Luckily, however, Myers knew the percipient personally and was also able to secure a confirmatory statement from her husband.

On June 9, 1885 the young woman went to bed feeling very

depressed. Unlike the existential vacuum which evoked the burning phantom of Kate Christie, this depression had a more immediate, though just as anguishing, cause. She had been summoned home only to learn of her father's death. Lying in bed, "the room became suddenly full of beautiful light, in the midst of which stood my father absolutely transfigured, clothed with brightness." Finally the figure receded and he and the light vanished. Why did this phantom glow?

It has often been argued that psychical phenomena are drastically affected by culture. Today, there is a noticeable lack of mediums, those psychics whose extrasensory abilities seem to reach out to bring communications from the dead. It has been argued that when mediumship was in its heyday during the last century, it was due to the fact that that period of time was still enveloped in Christian religious ethics where the concepts of the "soul" and "immortality" were culturally accepted. Thus, those with any extrasensory ability gathered material about the dead and passed it off in the mode of postmortem communications. Today, our new hedonism, astonishing scientific developments, and cultural revolution have wiped out the childlike devotion to religious authority that had always bound Western society. Today one hears so much about the magic of the mind that instead of using ESP abilities to prove immortality, our culture has induced those with this ability to project it toward telepathy, clairvoyance, and precognition. Since we no longer are interested in gaining proof of life after death, ESP no longer manifests in that form.

Can the reason apparitions were seen to glow be attributed to a cultural base? After all, any reader of the Bible will remember many accounts of angels of fire. In the book of Daniel (10:5–6) the narrator writes of lifting his eyes to see an apparition "whose loins were garbed with fine gold of Uphaz . . . his face as the appearance of lightning and his eyes as lamps of fire . . ." And who can forget the Psalmist who questions so poetically, "Who maketh his angels spirits and his ministers a flame of fire?"

Many would argue that the glowing of apparitions is merely a trick of the mind. Phantoms are expected to glow so when an apparitional presence manifests, through the extrasensory ability of the viewer, the mind also creates it as glowing. This adroit explanation may have some merit, but even today in a culture which can hardly be said to be preoccupied with spiritual values and doctrines, apparitions are still seen to glow, as the following recent cases indicate.

C. G. Jung admitted that his theory that apparitions were projections from the mind could not stand up against the combined testimony collected from different cultures and different areas. One such collection of cases, made in Switzerland in 1954–55, was submitted to Jung, who gave them to his assistant, Dr. Aniela Jaffé, to analyze. This led to Dr. Jaffé's book, *Apparitions and Precognition.*

One woman wrote of how she had lost her father to the strange kingdom of death and, like Frederic Myers's percipient, she had gone to bed, a solace for private mourning and mental disharmony. "It was just time for me to get up when I was overcome by terrible stomach colic and had to stay in bed. Suddenly I heard the door open and there were soft footsteps with a strange noise of knocking—I was alone at home and was rather frightened. Then the miracle happened—my beloved father came towards me, shining and lovely as gold, and transparent as mist. . . ."

Another narrator reported, "In 1926 I went to England. Suddenly one night my grandmother appeared to me, just as I knew her, but transparent and bright as the sun with a smile on her withered lips. . . . I knew I would never see my grandmother again on earth. . . . Two days later I heard from my family in Switzerland that my grandmother had died the night she appeared to bid me good-bye."

All in all, Dr. Jaffé reports that about ten percipients were struck by the radiance that accompanied the phantasmal presence. Dr. Jaffé also feels that this glowing has a cultural base. In her discussion of these cases the psychologist argues that radiance has always been associated with the divine. In fact, the entire history of man reveals an archetypal image of light accompanying or heralding divine presences and the manifestations of the "soul."

This argument leads to what I call the chicken-egg paradox in psychical research. So many times the argument is made that extrasensory phenomena are perceived in a certain fashion because of cultural and symbolic bias. For example, many report hearing divine and transcendental music when they die. Skeptics dispute the authenticity of psychic music because they believe that one is suggestionized into hearing such music because Biblical passages record welcoming choruses of angels. So it follows that during the out-of-the-body experience we see ourselves in an apparitional body because we have been led to believe that we have a soul-body which will survive death. These arguments can go on and on.

The chicken-egg paradox is the rebuttal to this inconsistency. Stated simply this principle goes something like this: In a case where a psychical phenomenon betrays a cultural influence, do we have the right automatically to assume that it was cultural heritage which led to this "illusion," or isn't it just as logical to believe that it was the psychical phenomenon that gave rise to the cultural tradition?

There is no way to refute this argument. There has been an encyclopedic amount of writing about man and his symbols. In fact, Jung's last work was on this topic. What is the source for all the archetypes in our cultures? Could it be that man was just trying to express the psychical? Certainly many symbols have a sexual base, as psychoanalysis has revealed. And certainly many symbols have similar psychological etiology. But when we talk of religious symbols, such as the light that accompanies the onset of the divine, as well as all the traditions of the dead returning to haunt or help the living, are these psychologically based traditions or are they the impact that empirical observations of the psychic have made on all men in all ages and in all cultures? Personally, I favor this theory.

Why, then, do apparitions seem to glow? Phantoms are, in my opinion, entities that are to some degree independent of the viewer. Edmund Gurney, the principal author of *Phantasms of the Living*, proposed that apparitions are merely a visualization of the telepathically received impulse. G. N. M. Tyrrell went beyond this simple explanation to theorize that both the sender and receiver of a telepathic thought might join forces and together form a mental image of an apparition. These hypotheses to not take into full account all the indications that apparitions have some sort of objectivity. They are seen collectively, reflect in mirrors, move objects, and are seen by animals. Clearly, although they might be creations of the mind, living or dead, they are somehow independent of it.

Yet, it is also clear that we perceive apparitions by a psychic sense, by some form of ESP. After all, often only one of a group may see an apparition and it may appear fully clothed. In many evidential cases of crisis apparitions, the evidence lies in the fact that the viewer was able to describe the clothes worn by the figure which were later found to be those in which the victim died or was injured. In other cases apparitions may be seen accompanied by visions of landscapes or other material objects. It is hard to believe that these extraneous visions have any objective qualities.

So it appears we are "seeing" an apparition. But we do not see it via the orthodox perception of sight. Sight is a physiological function, with the sensory organs serving as conveyors of information, and the mind often tricks the organs into taking in psychic perceptions as well. The many reports of glowing apparitions indicate that we are not seeing the figure by our normal sense of sight. Although it seems that we are viewing the phantom through our physical eyes, a clairvoyant type of sight is, in fact, intermingling with our sense organs. The object is spatially present although not physical enough to be ascertainable to normal sensory channels. Apparitions might be compared to infrared or ultraviolet rays which can be present and have an effect upon us, but we cannot see them.

The spatial presence of an apparition might then ignite the ESP ability of all its viewers. It might also be perceived congruently by one or more of the physical senses such as conventional sight or hearing. We do not see the force of magnetism as it raises a steel ball, but nonetheless, we know it is there through the testimony of our senses. Much is the same with apparitions. Although we see them clairvoyantly (or more correctly the presence of the apparition ignites our clairvoyance) our physical sight may see a door actually open or an object move if the phantom affects it. Our physical sight is not exercised until light affects the optic nerves. So it is that our clairvoyant vision is not affected until a psychic stimulus reaches it. However, this clairvoyance is revealing a spatially distinct and objective entity.

Phantoms are seen to glow not because our minds create this illusion, but because we are not seeing through a conventional physical organ. We are seeing through a different organ of sight which has its own laws of perception which may not be in accord with the physical senses although they may have very similar characteristics.

The theory that clairvoyant vision, when highly developed, may share common characteristics with physical sight was demonstrated by Dr. Hans Bender, a German psychologist who has now become Germany's leading parapsychologist. In 1933 Dr. Bender began investigating the paranormal ability of Fraulein D. In some of the tests, the psychic was supposed to try to visualize, through ESP, a letter printed on a card upon which Dr. Bender was concentrating. She later sketched all her impressions and visualizations that led up to the final visual reception of the letter. Bender then ran a group of tests with the same cards, but this time Fraulein D. looked at the letters directly. Bender used an apparatus that gradually increased the visibility of the letter on the card to the naked eye. Again Fraulein D. was asked to draw her purely visual perceptions as a vague object came into focus. By comparing the two sets of data, Bender hoped to ascertain if the reception of ESP in a gifted subject was similar to the laws of optics. In this case, the two sets of drawings were markedly similar.

A telling point can also be made in favor of this theory by checking reports of out-of-the-body experiences. Obviously during the out-of-the-body state the experiencer is not seeing through the organs of sight. When a person's consciousness travels over a great distance and reports correctly what it has seen, the physical eyes are not involved. Some researchers have argued that out-of-the-body experiences are really akin to dreams marked by telepathy and clairvoyance, but there is some evidence that can be used to counter this theory.

Karlis Osis is a Latvian-born psychologist who is now Director of Research for the ASPR. Dr. Osis is interested in resolving the question whether during the out-of-the-body experience the reporter is really spatially "seeing," or employing some form of telepathy or clairvoyance much as a blind man uses his cane to feel out his environment. Osis has had the good fortune to test his theory with a gifted subject, Ingo Swann, who has had many out-of-the-body experiences and has been willing to be tested under the watchful scientific eye of Dr. Osis.

So far work with him has been exploratory but the results have been significant. In these tests, Osis tried to determine if Swann could "see" physical objects in either of two ways—by conforming to the laws of optics or more vaguely by gaining only impressions via clairvoyance. Swann in his OOB state was asked to judge the various positions of objects in their proper perspective. If he looked through an opening in a box during this out-of-the-body state would he "see" only the contents that would be visible to the naked eye or would he also get vague clairvoyant impressions of all the contents?

For example, in one experiment Swann was supposed to "float up" in the room where he was being tested and report on the objects he saw on a shelf suspended from the ceiling. When Swann did this he reported the objects in correct perspective and proportion to each other.

Up until now all the evidence points to the fact that in his OOB state, Swann is seeing in the same way that one sees via the eyes. This would indicate that the consciousness has a psychic organ that is quite as highly evolved as physical vision. Clairvoyant impressions and visions are rarely so clearly defined as are the perceptions reported by Swann.

It is also extremely common that those undergoing an out-of-the-body experience see objects about them as glowing. This is parallel to how many people describe apparitions and their surroundings. This indicates that a person seeing an apparition is seeing it via the same mode of perception as someone in the out-of-the-body state where physical vision is clearly not possible.

Mrs. Caroline Larsen had an OOB experience while lying down in a darkened room. She was resting, soothed by some chamber music being performed in another room of her house. "Next I, I myself, was standing on the floor beside my bed looking down at my Physical Body—a strong whitish light—lighted up the room brilliantly."

Another woman reported how during an out-of-the-body experience she attempted to visit her sick husband in a neighboring room and found it "filled with a bright light."

These examples are typical and in other cases individuals undergoing the out-of-the-body experience report that every object they saw seemed to glow or that they themselves emitted light. It is highly likely that whatever perceptual apparatus is used during the OOB experience, this same form of extrasensory perception, which is probably much more highly evolved than the psychic perception of the normal mind, is invoked to see apparitions. This accounts for so many phantoms being seen as burning.

So far we have been discussing apparitions that glowed. Delving into the rich psychic heritage of ages past, we can find cases of phantoms that quite literally "burned" or were fiery. These cases are very old yet fascinating. A special study of them was made by an Italian psychical researcher, F. Zingaropoli.

If you were to visit the Convent of the Virgins at Naples you might be able to see a very strange sight—a sight not as strange, though, as the story behind it. Trespassing in the rector's cell on the fourth floor, you would see various pieces of religious art that so beautifully adorn these monuments of worship. One of these paintings is especially provoking. It is a painting of a crucifix with the imprints of two burning hands. As the story goes, a venerable Father of the mission decided to sleep in the cell where a dear friend had died. From that night on he was disturbed by manifestations which are so typical of the psychical—a visitation halfway between a vision and a dream. His dead friend continually appeared begging for confession. Finally, the persevering phantom pressed its hands on the painting of the crucifix leaving fiery imprints to prove its objective existence.

Another forgotten case of a burning apparition, seen in Rome in 1683, was found in records which formed a manuscript discovered in the archives of the Church of San Pontaleone and which was later moved to the Victor Emmanuel Central Library.

On March 11 Domenico Denza peacefully slept in his bedchamber. Suddenly he awoke to see a woman's figure. The phantom soon disappeared. That same month the apparition appeared three more times. In a sworn statement to Pope Innocent XI, Signor Denza wrote: "I saw that she was standing upright with the white mantle she previously wore, which covered her from the top of her head to the ground—she was of moderate stature, but the white mantle which she wore appeared so luminous that it seemed as though there were lighted torches under it, which emitted a dazzling light which illuminated the whole room."

The phantom tried to communicate with Denza, begging his pity, and "as she said this streaks of fire came towards me from her breast as though two bundles of tow had been lighted." Finally the apparition said, "Look where I touch" and vanished, as apparitions are in the habit of doing.

"After she had gone," Denza reported, "I remained languid and speechless for half-an-hour, then, as it pleased the Lord, having come somewhat to myself, I knocked on the door at the head of the bed, which led into my brother's room, and he immediately answered, and believing that some ill had happened to me he immediately lit the candle and came to my chamber; finding the door locked as usual he opened it from outside with the key, and on entering found me languid and pale—I asked him if he had seen any woman in the hall. He replied, 'What woman? Are you dreaming?' He went, however, to look, even under the covered table at the end of the hall. Then I asked him to look whether there was anything on the bed. He replied that there was nothing; then, looking more attentively, he said, with a surprised air, that the coverlet was burned, and in the middle of it was an imprint of a right hand. Having myself also seen it with great surprise, I dressed and went with him into his room. . . ."

Pope Innocent XI saw the imprint left by the burning hand and was very impressed. All the fingers were distinctly shown while the palm print was a little lighter than the dark burns imprinting the fingers.

The Reverend Father Joüet was a priest who was especially fascinated by these cases of fiery phantoms and, as with many clerics, his scholarly abilities led him into the labyrinthine domain of the paranormal. He began to catalogue cases of burning apparitions among which he discovered an old case titled "The Account of the real hand of the Rev. Father Panzini, Olivetian, November 1st, 1731."

Father Panzini was a venerable priest and after his death his friend, Isidore Gazole, hoped to receive some sign that his fellow priest still existed in spiritual form. One of the members of his church, Sister Claire-Isabella Formani, seemed receptive to psychic influences and it was through her that Father Gazole received the sign he so ardently desired.

During Mass the transparent figure of Father Panzini appeared to the Sister: "He pressed her arm, his other hand remaining on a sheet of paper, and on her arm as well as her chemise and tunic, and also on the paper with a double design, it left the imprint of the real, the very real hand of the said Rev. Father Abbé Panzini. . . ."

Father Joüet, like many Catholic clergy, was also interested in investigating claims of the miraculous. The Catholic Church has a long tradition of psychical investigations beginning with the writings of Cardinal Lambertini (later Pope Benedict XIV) who drew up elaborate and very accurate methods for analyzing what we today would call psychic phenomena. In fact, many early ecclesiastical authorities could be considered the first organized body of psychical researchers.

Father Joüet personally investigated a case of a fiery phantom which was supposed to have appeared at Ducey, France, in 1875. The apparition appeared to Jean de Sénéchal, who recognized the phantom as his wife who had recently died. The apparition left her burning fingerprints on her husband's nightcap.

Joüet was invited to investigate the case in 1905 by the local priest, Father Jean Hay. Before her death Mme. Sénéchal made her husband promise to say prayers for her. This promise was not carried out and soon Sénéchal's house was the focal point for haunting phenomena—shadows darted here and there, strange noises disturbed the peaceful bliss of sleep, and, finally, the apparition appeared "all aflame as though in a fire of burning oakum." The phantom again urged that prayers be said for her and laid her hand on her husband's nightcap, scorching it with her fingerprints.

Meanwhile a neighbor, Marie Tullet, who had derided her neighbor's complaints of psychic disturbances saw her entire garden aglow. As her garden glistened a female form appeared, as fiery as her garden, and then vanished along with the unearthly glow.

After Jean de Sénéchal carried out the request made of him and said the prayers for which the apparition earnestly petitioned, the strange sounds and visions ceased. Father Hay was, in fact, Sénéchal's grand-nephew and personally gathered the testimony.

Father Joüet continued to search out cases of imprints left by burning phantoms, collecting over ten additional incidents. All these cases are uniform even though they span a great many years, from 1696 to 1903.

It is easy to comfort ourselves with the thought that older generations lacked our scientific attitudes or our highly evolved intellectuality. Most investigators of psychical phenomena will no doubt tell the inquirer that only with the founding of the Society for Psychical Research in 1882 was the study of the supernatural approached in an objective and scientific manner. Still, it was the first parapsychologists who finally showed, in the mass of religious dogma, human testimony, legend and superstition, that there was something genuinely worth studying. To those who do not hold such an opinion these old cases of purgatorial phantoms hold no challenge. They were simply the result of exaggeration, religious indoctrination, and fallibility of human testimony and credulity.

It is not so easy to dismiss these cases, though. For one thing, each of these phantoms left an imprint of its visit. The imprints were subjected to the scrutiny of Church authorities who were impressed by them. The Church then, as now, was always reticent about admitting the manifestation of the spiritual and, in true parapsychological tradition, rarely certified an occult occurrence unless rigid standards of evidence were met.

We can offer no explanation as to what these burning phantoms were. In many respects they were similar to the type of occurrences reported today. They appeared and disappeared, they were often recognized as phantoms of the dead, and they often made requests of the living. The mind is a mysterious thing. But nature is even more so!

SEVEN

wild hauntings!

The term "haunted house" has amassed many connotations down through the centuries. To some, a haunted house evokes a picture of a gloomy, foreboding, half-deserted mansion inhabited only by a ghostly tenant forever walking its halls. Others might envision a glorious gothic cathedral where worship is complemented by ghostly monks. Or a cold but inviting British castle complete with friendly and well-wishing wraiths.

How such representations developed is a mystery. It is certain though that the glamor and atmosphere often associated with haunted houses are based on fictional stories about ghosts where effect and drama take precedence over fact or accuracy. Nonetheless, hauntings do represent a wide range of effects. Some, like the Morton ghost, consist of merely a phantom. Others include the movement of objects, mysterious fires, sounds and smells, and so on. In fact, some manifestations are so violent that they become, quite literally, "wild hauntings."

Calvados Castle is a gloomy, medieval castle in France. A rambling estate, it hardly looks like a prime prospect for human dwelling. To look at it one might think, "What a perfect place for a ghost." To be sure, it is! In 1875 the owner and residents of the castle began recording odd manifestations that occurred in the house. The family was so disturbed by ghostly sounds and other activities that they secretly placed threads across the openings to the castle in the hope of obtaining some indication that intruders were entering. Even though noises still were heard, the threads were never broken. Obviously the disturbances came solely from within the castle. The household included the owners, M. and Mme. de X., their son, and his tutor, Abbé Y.; the coachman Emile and servants, Auguste, Amelina, and Celina.

On Wednesday, October 13, 1875, M. de X. began keeping a record of the strange events at Calvados Castle. That night the Abbé was alone in his room when a series of raps were heard on his wall and a candlestick on the mantelpiece was moved by an invisible force. The terror-stricken Abbé rang for M. de X., who found that an armchair, which he had securely fastened to the floor, had moved by itself toward the fireplace.

For the next two days violent poundings on the castle wall continued. Armed, M. de X. ransacked his own castle only to discover that the intruder was either invisible or escaped him at every turn. Resting from the ordeal the Abbé and Amelina heard phantom footsteps in the hall. Later more poundings rocked the castle.

These raps finally ceased a few days later. But the cessation of hostilities proved to be only a time to rearm and plan the next attack. On October 31 Calvados Castle erupted into a nightmare of ghostly sounds and disturbances. M. de X. recorded in his diary: "A very disturbed night. It sounded as if someone went up the stairs with superhuman speed from the ground floor, stamping his feet. Arriving on the landing, he gave five heavy blows, so strong that objects suspended on the wall rattled in their places. Then it seemed as if a heavy anvil or a big log had been thrown on the wall, so as to shake the house. Nobody could say whence came these blows. Everybody got up and assembled in the passage of the first floor. We made a minute inspection but found nothing. We went to bed, but more noises obliged us to get up again. We could only go to rest at about three o'clock."

Their rest was short-lived, for the next day the unearthly events intensified. That evening everyone was awakened by the sound of a body rolling down the stairway. Reaching the bottom of the stairs, the entity pounded violently on the wall of one of the castle's rooms. Every day the sounds continued, blows rocked the castle, and mysterious footsteps gruesomely portrayed the phantom visitant. "At 2 A.M.," wrote M. de X., "some being rushed at top speed up the stairs from the entrance hall to the first floor . . . with a loud noise of tread which had nothing human about it. Everybody heard it. It was like two legs deprived of their feet and walking on the stumps."

By mid-November the haunting entered its second phase. So far the family had been disturbed by unnatural sounds. Now, it seemed, the entity wished to speak. On November 10, the household was once more the scene of violent noises which culminated in an unearthly scream: ". . . everybody heard a long shriek, and then another, as of a woman outside calling for help. At 1:45 [A.M.] we suddenly heard three or four loud cries in the hall, and then on the staircase."

These shrieks finally enveloped the entire castle. Hundreds of cries, screams, and moans were heard echoing through the barren halls. Sometimes voices, weeping and moaning, called from the halls; at other times stifled cries filled the cellar. These wailings became so violent that M. de X. recorded in his diary, "It is no longer the cry of a weeping woman, but shrill, furious, despairing cries, the cries of demons or the damned."

Not only were voices heard, but the castle furniture became animated—windows opened by themselves, beds overturned, chairs shifted over the floor, and Bibles were torn and desecrated. Even attacks on persons occurred. "Mme. de X., hearing a noise in the Abbé's room, goes up there, followed by the latter. She heard a movement in the room, and put out her right hand to open the latch of the door. Before she could touch it she saw the key turn quickly in the lock and detach itself, hitting her left hand. The Abbé witnessed this. The blow was so strong that the place was sensitive and visible for two days." That night blows pounded on Mme. de X.'s door so wildly and malignantly that she envisioned the wall collapsing. The thundering sounds continued all over the castle for days upon days.

The new year brought only new manifestations—even more terrible blows; it seemed the whole house shook; and there were shrieks like a bull roaring. The manifestations were growing more and more sinister, violent, and dangerous. On January 26, the entire castle "was shaken twenty times"; every floor was wracked by hammerings; it sounded like cattle were stampeding through the castle; screams and cries resounded and finally menacing laughter terrified the residents. The family could stand no more.

A priest was called in to read the rites of exorcism and the tenants placed religious medals and medallions throughout the house, and finally the manifestations ceased.

The hauntings at Calvados Castle represent the most violent and malicious case of its type I know of. Indeed the reader might believe that these records seem more of an excerpt from a scenario and might well seem more apropos in Shirley Jackson's fine novel *The Haunting of Hill House*, than in a serious parapsychological publication. But the fact that some awful manifestations tormented the victims of Calvados Castle rests on the unusually strong testimony of the witnesses. M. J. Morice was fascinated by the case and actively tried to investigate it some years after the disturbances had ceased. He was able to read over the firsthand accounts in the diaries of M. and Mme. de X. and also locate the Abbé, who by then had become a parish priest in Normandy. The Abbé wrote out a long deposition attesting to his experiences at the castle and in which he also revealed that the exorcism rites were not the finale of that horrible infestation.

Shortly after the exorcism one last violent blow seemed to terminate the haunting. However, the next morning the residents found that all the medals and crosses they had placed throughout the castle had been stolen or had vanished. A few days later, even though the castle was finally enveloped in peace, these medals suddenly materialized out of thin air and mysteriously fell on a small desk where Mme. de X. was writing. After this display of sacrilege more blows and violence erupted. Whether or not peace finally quieted the menacing halls of Calvados Castle is not a matter of record.

In the Calvados haunting no phantoms were actually seen although their unholy voices and trampings were heard. In some cases of a similar nature actual phantoms are seen during the outbreaks of haunting phenomena. I was able personally to investigate one such outbreak in 1973. In this case objects were displaced, sounds heard, and phantoms seen. Unfortunately, I never witnessed any unusual occurrence, but I was able to inverview several people who did.

On February 2, I was at my desk writing. The telephone is often the scourge of the writer when its shrill wail interrupts the train of thought so arduously being set to paper. True to form I was in the midst of working on a rather complex problem when the phone interrupted my finally jelling ideas. Throwing down my pen and picking up the phone, I was delightfully surprised to find that my caller was not the usual phone soliciter or advice seeker but Dr. Thelma Moss, a psychologist on the staff of the UCLA Neuropsychiatric Institute. The call banished any feelings of annoyance at my having been roused from my desk.

Dr. Moss told me that earlier that morning the Institute had received a frantic call from a woman who lived in one of the small communities that comprise the San Fernando Valley. The woman reported odd psychical disturbances and desperately wanted someone to come out to talk over the problem with them. Since I lived close by Dr. Moss asked if I would like to check into the matter. I phoned the family, whom I shall call the Carters in this summary, and visited them that afternoon. That evening I returned to the house with my colleague Raymond Bayless, and we recorded all the testimony on tape. After the second interview I kept in phone contact with the family in case of any new development.

The Carters were a fairly large middle-class Roman Catholic family. Mr. Carter was a Brazilian-born civil engineer and his wife was the intelligent and attractive mother of six children. One child was away from home during the period which encompassed the outbreaks, so in essence the family consisted of five children: Carol, seventeen, and her younger sister Sharon, sixteen, who had witnessed most of the phenomena. Another daughter, Pauline, age eleven, also had some strange experiences. The two sons who were the main witnesses of the phantoms were Stan, fourteen and Mark, thirteen.

Before reporting on the experiences of this family I should point out a few things about them. First, during our investigation we took the testimony of several family members and at no time was any of the testimony contradictory. Both Mr. and Mrs. Carter struck us as good, reliable witnesses and the children seemed a bit frightened though interested in the happenings that plagued their home.

The prelude to this haunting-type infestation was in November 1972. Pauline saw a stuffed toy dog with floppy cloth ears, which sits on her dresser in her room, move by itself. Two weeks later, while she was holding the toy, the little stuffed animal ripped from her hands and hit the wall adjoining her bed. Her sister Sharon was in the room with her and witnessed this occurrence.

During the ensuing months several family members heard unaccountable footsteps and breathing in the house. Two nights before I was called into the case, Carol had heard footsteps and breathing coming from the central hall of the house. She immediately thought a prowler had gotten in, but composing herself, she rose from her bed and entered the hallway. Although she saw nothing she continued through the hallway and woke her mother. Mrs. Carter had not heard the mysterious sounds but Stan and Mark had.

Although Mrs. Carter missed out on witnessing this event she did have some unnerving experiences of her own. Mrs. Carter struck us as a very prudent housewife and mother. The old cliché "a woman's work is never done" seemed to suit her very well. True to form she reported that shortly before calling in an investigator she was engaged in kitchen chores while all the rest of the household were still asleep. Her only company was a portable radio to which she listens as she goes about her work. Mrs. Carter was startled when suddenly the radio switched stations and volume, from the gentle background music to which she usually listens to a wild jazz program. Interrupting her chores for a second, she diligently reset the radio but as soon as her back was turned, the radio switched to another station again.

Sharon also had problems with the radio. She, however, does not seem to have her mother's patience and immediately turned the troublesome set off. However the radio had a mind of its own, it seems, for it adroitly turned itself back on. On another occasion Sharon actually saw the radio knobs turn by themselves.

So far the family had heard phantom sounds but nothing had been seen. This was soon to change. The night before my arrival on the scene Mark had seen a shadowlike form in his room. He saw the shadow dart across his room and disappear into Sharon's. Mark thought the figure was a burglar, an impression which was strengthened when he heard shuffling sounds coming from his sister's closet. Stan had also seen a phantom figure early one morning. Half asleep he saw a form which looked to him like a man in a hat and cape who stared at him. He thought the form was his father and spoke to it. When the figure did not answer he became a bit puzzled; the form just drifted out of the room.

Meanwhile Sharon woke up the next morning to behold a strange sight. Something *had* been in her closet. Clothes were in disarray and all the hangers which were not draped by articles of apparel were wedged at a 45-degree angle upward between the clothes, in a rather bizarre fashion. The family had not touched the closet and when I arrived a bit later that day I was able to see this curious sight. It was as though someone had very carefully taken the hangers, pulled them out from the closet pointing upward, secured them in this puzzling position, and left.

Later that morning the phantom was seen again, but this time by several members of the family collectively. Both Sharon and Carol saw two apparitional forms resembling feet moving back and forth in the hallway. They called Mrs. Carter to the scene, but she reported seeing only an "amorphous form." This form traveled through the house until Carol grabbed a crucifix and ordered the "thing" to depart. The phantom vanished.

One peculiarity cropped up from this presence. Carol reported that she attempted to walk through the phantom. As she made contact with it she said it felt as though she had come into contact with a charge of static electricity, her skin prickled, and the hair on her arms stood on end. This was a rather unusual report and at the time I did not take much note of it. Verification and corroboration of the incidents was the most important consideration at the time, since I was making only an initial investigation. However, some time later I came across a curious parallel to Carol's experience, one so close that it is rather remarkable. I was reading a report of an outbreak of psychic phenomena plaguing a house in Detroit. The case had come to the attention of W. G. Roll, who is project director of the Psychical Research Foundation in Durham, North Carolina. Bill Roll has been an active investigator of hauntings and kindred phenomena and has been a friend of mine for some years. The case was reported in his new book *The Poltergeist* and although the evidence in the case is not very compelling, there were some odd reports that cannot be easily dismissed. Roll asked a friend, John Buta, to investigate the matter until he was able to get there from Durham, North Carolina, to handle things himself. Buta phoned Roll shortly after to report an odd experience. One of the family reported seeing two apparitions and Buta himself suddenly saw a "misty shape about three feet off the floor and six by eight inches in size." Buta touched the misty area and, as Roll writes, "When he moved his hand back and forth across the area, he noticed that the hairs stood up as if affected by static electricity." An interesting parallel indeed!

The fact that the Carters' phantom evaporated did not stop the eerie manifestations, and the rest of the morning was the scene of one inexplicable event after another. It began as Mark was sitting in his room with Pauline, listening to the accursed radio. The "ghost in the machine" once more played its gremlinlike prank and raised the volume to a roar. This was the final straw—everyone was so unnerved that all the members of the family who were present in the house huddled together in Mrs. Carter's bedroom. While all the children were in Mrs. Carter's sight the radio suddenly stopped playing. When they investigated they found that the cord had been pulled from the wall socket. By this time a relative of Mrs. Carter had phoned UCLA, which contacted me. By a typical irony of fate, there I was casually writing at my desk, while only a few miles away an outbreak of psychic phenomena was exploding like an angry volcano.

By the time I arrived in the afternoon the phenomena had just about burned out. This is not odd. Outbreaks such as these are usually short-lived, and my job seemed to be more of a post-mortem examination than an active investigation. Before my arrival a few more incidents had occurred, including the toilet flushing by itself and its tank top being displaced. I returned and spent the evening at the house with Mr. Bayless but as usual the family soon found us more interesting than their haunting and nothing occurred during our stay, or for that matter ever since.

In short, the Carters' problem was diagnosed to be not a conventional haunting, but a poltergeist. As is obvious the word "poltergeist" is German and roughly translated means "noisy ghost." Several cases of hauntings have been cited in this book and follow some sort of plan—they are long and drawn-out affairs, manifest usually in visual or auditory forms, and seem bound to a certain house or area. Poltergeists represent the other end of the haunting spectrum. They are short-lived, rarely lasting over a month or two; usually manifest by physical demonstrations such as moving objects, breaking kitchenware with fearful noises; and seem to be bound not to a place but to center around an individual and may even follow if he seeks shelter in a neighboring home.

Poltergeists are rather diversified creatures and have an arsenal of manifestations. If one were to find himself in the midst of a poltergeist outbreak one could expect several of the following events to occur: objects have been known to fly and be propelled at people; mysterious rocks or other missiles might attack the house; poundings on the walls often accompany these displays; objects might mysteriously disappear and then reappear; fires have been known to ignite spontaneously; and on rarer occasions voices are heard and phantoms seen.

The poltergeist is a much more dynamic and active phenomenon than conventional hauntings. One of the most unusual characteristics of the poltergeist is that it usually centers on one individual. Although the phenomenon will attack an entire house, its manifestations more often than not will occur in the presence of a particular member of the family who will also often be the prime target of the poltergeist. Luckily, there have been few serious injuries due to poltergeist mischief, but that is not to say that severe personal harm has not been caused by them. There are a few such cases known, but they are rather rare.

For many years poltergeist cases were frowned upon by parapsychologists. The reason is not hard to fathom. The fact that these displays often center on an individual is suggestive of fraud. This is even more likely since in most cases the poltergeist percipient has been a child or youth. It is also true that fraud has been uncovered in a number of poltergeist cases. It was easy, as a consequence, to dismiss all such phenomena as being due to malobservation, trickery, or perfectly natural causes.

Or was it? Despite the climate of extreme conservatism that surrounds the study of poltergeist phenomena a few psychical researchers steadfastly held to the fact that they had personally witnessed poltergeist outbreaks that could not have been faked. Cesare

Lombroso, an Italian criminologist who turned all his attention to psychical research later in his life, visited a poltergeist-ridden inn in Turin. Alone in the cellar he watched as wine bottles moved by themselves, falling but not breaking, exploding, etc. Finally, a servant boy was dismissed from the inn and the poltergeist disappeared. In Great Britain the physicist Sir William Barrett had a rare exchange with a poltergeist that was rampantly banging on the walls in a little country house. Barrett tried to communicate with the rapper and asked the entity to rap out how many fingers he held outstretched in his pocket concealed from view. The poltergeist was most accommodating and correctly rapped out the number and continued to do so as the experiment was repeated over and over.

Parapsychologists have always been wary of human testimony, even when it came from their own colleagues. It was not the testimony of men such as Barrett and Lombroso that once again prompted parapsychologists to reevaluate poltergeist reports, but some extraordinary developments at Duke University. Dr. J. B. Rhine had already set the scientific community aflame by showing statistically that ESP was a factor in his guessing experiments. This controversy had not yet calmed down before Rhine revealed that he had another scientific bombshell up his sleeve.

Some people have always claimed that they had ESP, that they had access to or could influence another person's thoughts. Just as peculiar, some individuals insist that, by purely mental means, they have the ability to move or affect physical objects. This claim fascinated Rhine and when a gambler insisted that he had the ability to influence the fall of dice Rhine put his claims to the test. Could a subject make dice come up with one face more often than another at a statistically significant rate? Was there such a thing as mind over matter? Hundreds of tests were run during the next several years. In some of them the subject "willed" a specific die face or pairs to come up. In others the dice were dropped from a chute mechanically and the subject "willed" them to land in a certain position.

The results were not as staggering as the ESP results but were no less controversial. It did appear that somehow some energy, perhaps engendered by the living agent's will, was affecting these objects while in motion. Just as claims of ESP were finally obtaining scientific credence, so mind over matter, or psychokinesis, also could be demonstrated in a scientific laboratory.

The results of these tests led parapsychologists to consider once again if claims of poltergeist cases might not harbor hidden truths. It seems that with so many observations by eminent researchers who had witnessed poltergeist outbreaks this curiosity was rather tardy in getting attention. But organized parapsychology has always been a reserved animal and Rhine's laboratory experiments gave the impetus to researchers to check again into claims of violent physical displays. For once, it seemed, psychical researchers had some concrete scientific data to which they could point when accused of "chasing ghosts."

It strikes me, however, that the logic of this interest in mind over matter was a bit backward. It was claimed that the evidence for PK (as laboratory psychokinesis is abbreviated) lent credibility to claims of poltergeist visitations. It has always been my opinion that the opposite was more the case—that the rich and well-evidenced reports of the poltergeist gave credence to Rhine's experiments and those of his colleagues as being due to a psychical force and not to some error in their experimental techniques. This argument is not an important one really, and despite the puzzles one often finds in studying the fascinating history of parapsychology, it is a historical fact that the Duke PK experiments heralded the birth of a new interest in the poltergeist.

Before embarking on a discussion of phantoms seen during poltergeist outbreaks I would like to outline a recent typical example of this type of wild haunting. As previously mentioned, one of the leading investigators of poltergeistery in the United States is W. G. Roll. Originally from Denmark, Roll was educated in the United States and England before turning his attention full-time to parapsychology. Roll has had the good fortune actually to have seen a poltergeist or two in action as in the following investigation at Olive Hill, Kentucky.

I can remember very vividly the stir this case made when Roll first announced that he had witnessed the events himself. The scene was the 1969 Convention of the Parapsychological Association held in New York. The conference had not been overly stimulating—ESP tests were reported, methodology argued, and so on. I was sitting in a rather uncomfortable seat at the rear of the assembly room when Bill Roll caught everyone's attention with the following report:

The Callihan home had been the scene of objects moving, glasses breaking, furniture overturned, and the usual poltergeist gymnastics. During this outbreak Mrs. Callihan saw a phantom which she thought she recognized as a previous occupant of the poltergeist-infected house. When Roll heard about the case he sent a colleague, John Stump, to hold down the fort until he arrived. By this time the Callihans and their five children had moved into a new house to be free from this psychic plague. Despite the move more disturbances bombarded them. Furniture again toppled over, pictures hurled from the walls, objects flew across rooms.

Stump was able to see some of the activities himself and on one occasion saw two bottles and a glass jar slide across a counter. Another time he pointed to a chair only to have it somersault before him while no one was in its immediate vicinity. During this period phantoms were once again seen. Grandmother Callihan scurried from her bed one night during the investigation claiming that a large white phantom, like a "large white Catholic nurse," had entered her room and moved toward her. Immediately after the report of the phantom more objects began to move.

Finally Roll arrived on the scene. It didn't take long for the investigator to witness the poltergeist in action: "At five minutes past midnight on Monday, December 16, 1968, I was walking behind 12-year-old Roger Callihan as he entered the kitchen of his home. When he came to the sink, he turned toward me and at that moment the kitchen table, which was on his right, jumped into the air, rotated about 45 degrees and came to rest on the backs of the chairs that stood around it, with all four legs off the floor. It happened in a twinkling of an eyelid."

Unfortunately, Roll's investigation of this promising case had to be aborted. The family felt that the arrival of the parapsychologists had only antagonized "the spook," so Roll and his colleagues had to leave "the demon in Olive Hill."

In the Olive Hill poltergeist case a phantom was reported on at least two occasions. The appearance of phantoms during such cases is not common, but it is certainly known in the literature of the field. Poltergeists, like many forms of psychical disturbances, also include an experience of phantoms.

A phantom was seen during a recent case in Iceland. The Einarsson family were the center of these manifestations as objects shifted position and were displaced. It was a typical poltergeist. One night a daughter, Sigurdborg, woke up and went into her parents' room. There, to her amazement, she saw the phantom of an old man walk up to a table in the dark room and vanish. What is so interesting in this case is that it was this very table that had been repeatedly moved by the poltergeist.

What do phantoms have to do with poltergeists? Are they merely another one of the various phenomena or are they more intricately involved in it? To answer this question general consideration must first be given to explaining what we think a poltergeist is.

Long ago poltergeists were explained as being either demons or spirits of the dead. Today, however, researchers such as Roll and Hans Bender have been able to make sophisticated psychological analyses of poltergeist cases. We said before that poltergeists often focus on an individual and through psychological testing Roll has found that a recurring pattern of mental distress is present with these individuals. Usually pent-up hostility is present which has been repressed and has found no means of expression. We express hostility in many ways. The most overt is of course verbal expression. But there are other ways as, for instance, in what psychology calls "acting out," where a young child gets so angry at his parents that he rips pictures of adults out of his coloring book. It is now generally assumed that a poltergeist represents a nonverbal form of expression for hostility. Instead of the agent physically throwing an object or smashing a dish, a psychokinetic force does the job for him. Generally, the agent is not aware that he is responsible for the odd occurrences which are just as terrifying to him as to the rest of the people involved. During Roll's investigations of several poltergeist cases this type of pent-up hostility and frustration was found. It was also determined that many occurrences transact closer to the agent than to any other member of the family and that when the agent is not present at all there is a marked decline in the incidents of poltergeist nuisance.

This theory is now a generally accepted explanation as to what a poltergeist is and what causes it. The actual mechanics are, of course, still a mystery.

Not everyone, though, is really happy with this explanation. For example, what about phantoms seen during poltergeist attacks? In the Carter case which I investigated many phenomena were precipitated around the time that shadowlike apparitions were seen. In the Icelandic case the table which was moved several times by the poltergeist seemed to be an object of attention not only of the poltergeist but of a visible phantom as well. In other cases a phantom seems to be present although it may not be seen. For example, many objects do not fly through the air, but seem to be carried by an invisible invader—the object moves unnaturally, much slower than a thrown object would travel, and even makes 45-degree or 90-degree turns to enter a room. Dr. Ian Stevenson shares the opinion that this type of odd action is difficult to explain as being due to a PK force. Stevenson feels that abrupt changes of speed and trajectory cannot be explained by a force projected by the agent but that, in some poltergeist cases, an independent entity might be the source of the disturbance. Stevenson's opinion is certainly not a new one in psychical research.

Phantoms represent this very type of independent agency. Could a phantom be the cause of a poltergeist disturbance? And more important, what is the source of the phantom? Can the existence of phantoms be reconciled with all the new evidence that poltergeists are projections from living agents?

To explain this problem we must once again turn to the phenomena of the out-of-the-body experience. It has long been known that certain individuals who have undergone this experience have claimed that on certain occasions they were seen as an apparition by another person. In the first chapter I cited the case of S. H. Beard, who projected an image that was so physical that two witnesses saw it at the same time. There is an old occult tradition that man possesses a "double" that can be projected, and the data on the out-of-the-body experience lends some validity to this claim. Whether or not man has a superphysical body is a question too complex to enter into at this point. However, the question remains, if one can project an image or consciousness of himself, can that form move physical objects? If there is evidence for this, then there is evidence that a person can project his consciousness via an out-of-the-body experience draped as a semi-physical phantom and this might affect poltergeist phenomena. There is some evidence for this.

Lucien Landau is a British businessman who has had many psychic experiences. Some of these have been shared by his wife, Eileen. Among Eileen's experiences have been numerous out-of-the-body experiences. On one night in September 1955 they planned an experiment to see if Eileen, who slept in a separate room, could move a physical object. As Mr. Landau reports, the results were amazing:

> I woke up suddenly, it was dawn, and there was just about enough light coming in through curtains to enable me to read . . . [there] stood the figure of Eileen, facing northwest, and looking straight ahead towards the window. The figure was wearing a night dress, its face was extremely pale, almost white. The figure was moving slowly backwards towards the door, but it was otherwise motionless, it was not walking. . . . I got out of bed and followed. I could then clearly see the moving figure, which was quite opaque and looking like a living person, but for the extreme pallor of her face, and at the same time the head of Eileen, asleep in her bed, the bedclothes rising and falling as she breathed. I followed the figure which moved all the time backwards, looking straight ahead, but apparently not seeing me. I kept my distance and ultimately stood in the door of a spare bedroom, when the figure . . . suddenly vanished. There was no visible effect on Eileen, who did not stir and whose rhythm of breathing remained unchanged.
>
> I moved quietly back to my room . . . and found a rubber toy dog, which belonged to Eileen and which stood on a small chest of drawers.

Eileen Landau similarly reported how she woke up in the out-of-the-body state: "I lifted my rubber toy dog, and I remember taking it through the door, across the landing, to the other room but do not remember actually *walking*. I did not find the dog heavy, or difficult to hold. I have no recollection of what I finally did with it." She saw her husband but could not remember what occurred afterward.

This striking case is very suggestive that phantoms of the living can move physical objects. This claim is not novel and many who have undergone the out-of-the-body experience have reported how they were able to move a physical object. Sylvan Muldoon had hundreds of experiences which he chronicled in his book *The Pro-*

jection of the Astral Body. On one occasion he reported how he set a metronome in motion during an out-of-the-body excursion.

It is not hard then to share the opinion that poltergeist movements might be due to a phantom and that this phantom might be the projection from a living person. There are natural criticisms to this theory though. A skeptic would argue that in cases of out-of-the-body travel the consciousness is located with the apparitional body and the physical body is usually inert. How can my theory hold water since there is a marked decline of poltergeist activity when the physical body is asleep, or in any other form of unconsciousness, which is when most out-of-the-body experiences occur?

This criticism is fair, but can be rebutted. For example, apparitions of the living have been seen even though the agent was in a normal conscious state and no way aware that his phantom had been liberated. One man who has had some experience with this bizarre variant of astral projection is the Australian philosopher and writer Arthur Osborn, who has written several fascinating books on mysticism, metaphysics, and parapsychology. Unlike the usual philosophizing that one has to wade through in reading about psychical research much of Osborn's views and opinions is based on personal experience. Unlike some linguistic philosophers who argue from symbolic logic, connotation and denotation of terms, and argument, Osborn's refreshing approach is based on empirically collected data. With the philosopher Whitehead, Osborn shares the tenet that human experience is more important than words or argument.

On one occasion Osborn was ill with influenza yet perfectly awake. While he was lying in his bed an odd manifestation occurred to his wife in another room of their home. Going about her chores, she suddenly saw the figure of her husband, perfectly naked, dancing in front of her. Now this is hardly an activity in which a philosopher usually indulges, and Osborn reports that his wife must have thought that the flu had developed into delirium. Obviously Mrs. Osborn had taken the naked figure to be her husband yet all the while he was confined to bed with his illness.

In this case, even though the agent was absolutely awake, his phantom was seen and mistaken as very lifelike. Osborn himself also records that once while ascending his staircase he met his own double face to face. Again, he had no knowledge that any phantom was loose.

These cases suggest that it is very possible for a living person to project a semi-physical phantom while still being unaware that he is the agent of any psychical phenomenon.

In order to explore further my theory that phantoms seen during poltergeist cases are actually projections from the living that represent either some form of "astral body" or physical and independent creations by the agent for the purpose of inciting a poltergeist, let us take a look at one poltergeist case in which a phantom of a living girl was actually observed more than once to be the perpetrator of the disturbances.

Brook House is not an especially interesting name, nor was it a specially interesting house. It was a rather drab three-story dwelling with one main entrance that was typical of the Victorian times during which it was built. Despite its utter homeliness Brook House was the center for one of the most active poltergeists whose records have come down to us.

What we know of Brook House comes to us through a chief witness, Ralph Hastings, who was the fiancé of a young lady who resided in the haunted building. Hastings encountered odd occurrences at the house on so many occasions that he recorded them in his diary. Later he edited these notes and turned them over to W. T. Stead, a journalist whose main interest had turned to psychical studies. Stead, in turn, published them in a special issue of his "Review of Reviews," devoted completely to psychic matters.

Hastings witnessed not only typical poltergeist tricks but phantoms as well and these apparitions seemed linked to his fiancée, Miss B. In fact, it was through this bizarre phantom that he first learned that Brook House was the hunting ground of ghostly phenomena: " . . . I approached the house from Church Lane, I happened to glance at the window to the right on the second floor. There I saw to my astonishment the apparent figure of Miss B. standing partially dressed, arranging her hair and looking intently at me. On entering the house I was shown into the drawing-room, which was on the right hand side of the door, the dining-room being on the left. I found Miss B. sitting reading!" Miss B. had been sitting there all the while. Upon being questioned Miss B. admitted that her home was a stronghold of uncanny events.

Hastings hit upon an old law of psychic phenomena when he tried to comfort his distraught fiancée. ''Nothing happens when you are expecting it,'' he said. As any investigator of hauntings knows, Hastings's comment couldn't be truer, but the poltergeist is a notoriously ill-behaving entity and immediately after Hastings's remark all the bells in the house were set pealing. He was unnerved but curious. His nervousness was the stronger emotion and it was not until the next day that he returned to the house with a mutual friend. Since the house was stiflingly hot the pair flung open a second-story window. Later the two discovered that the window had been shut. Hastings returned to the room, reopened the window, and joined his companion in the garden. While there the two suddenly saw a phantom appear at the window.

''Presently, to our horror, a figure appeared resembling Miss B. yet most unlike her; its fearful eyes were gazing at me without movement and totally expressionless.'' Miss B. had also seen the phantom and fainted while the phantom was in Hastings's full view. It began to dissolve until only phantom hands remained which moved the window. The phantom resembled Miss B. but also her deceased sister as well.

Two days later Hastings secured the services of a priest to exorcise the house. Unlike Calvados Castle the services were totally inefficacious, for immediately after the service, doors slammed shut from no apparent cause, frightening the occupants badly. During the next days quite a variety of phenomena rocked Brook House. While Hastings was visiting one day a tray was scattered in the room though no one was near it; voices were heard calling and crying; Miss B's hair was singed.

This last phenomenon brings to mind the recent case of the late Bishop Pike. Pike encountered a poltergeist after his son's death by suicide. After this crushing emotional blow he began to be the focal point of odd poltergeist displays including displaced objects, clocks reset in a weird fashion, and other similar events. Pike and some friends who had taken an interest in these phenomena visited the Cambridge apartment where the youth had spent the last emotionally charged days before his suicide. During one of these visits a young woman with them uttered a cry and Pike and the others saw that something had singed her hair.

What the ultimate fate of Brook House was is a mystery. In our own time Rosalind Heywood, a sensitive and vice-president of the SPR, visited Brook House, but her investigation did not uncover anything new. Edmund Gurney also had been interested in Brook House but never seems to have gotten around to an in-depth consideration of it.

Who was the phantom of this wild haunting?

It is clear that the apparition represented Miss B. Although in his report Hastings mentioned that the phantom also had a strong family resemblance to a dead sister, the similarity to Miss B. herself was so great that Hastings mistook the phantom for her. Any reader of the report will realize that Hastings and Miss B. were on very familiar terms (by Victorian standards) so such an error would not be a likely one on Hastings's part. I think that it is fair to conclude that the phantom was some sort of projection or double of Miss B., who seemed to be the center of the poltergeist activity.

In other cases, too, phantoms can possibly be traced to living agents. For example, in the Carter case which so fascinated me when I investigated it, Stan saw a shadowy figure enter his room one morning and said that it seemed to be wearing some sort of hat. Mrs. Carter told us that her husband was in the habit of waking the children up in the morning, surprising them with funny hats. However, Mr. Carter strongly disclaimed any involvement in this incident. Could the phantom have been his double?

That these phantoms are responsible for some of the poltergeist displays is indisputable. In the Carter case the strongest incidents of objects being moved occurred close to the time the phantoms were sighted. At Brook House a phantom was seen to close a window, one of the most common psychokinetic effects that occurred there. In the Icelandic poltergeist case briefly outlined earlier, a phantom was seen as it stood by a table which was habitually moved. In all these cases it is obvious that the phantom was not just another in the poltergeist's repertoire of unnerving productions, but a perpetrator of them. Does this solve the mystery of why objects have been known to float or change trajectory as if hoisted by an invisible carrier?

Perhaps it also supplies the clue to what animates wild hauntings.

EIGHT

haunted houses today

If poltergeists can be typified as short-lived and violent, more conventional haunted houses might alternately be described as perennial, subtle, and even placid. The fact that poltergeists are so violent is quite a help to the psychical researcher. The fact that objects are hurled about one atop another, and crockery shattered while the poltergeist is rampant makes observation and study easy. All one needs to do is sit and wait.

In 1965 a newspaper in Bremen, Germany, reported that a noisy ''ghost'' was rattling glasses, vases, and porcelain figures in a small china shop. Since the ghost had caused severe damage and breakage the police had been called in. The police were just as ill-fated as the proprietors in handling the situation, but when Heiner, a fifteen-year-old apprentice, was sent home from the shop the events subsided. Two days later Dr. Hans Bender was summoned to the scene by the reports. It was not until the next year, however, that he witnessed the poltergeist firsthand. By this time Heiner was working as a maintenance man at a newly built school. One of his duties was to insert plastic plugs and screws into the basement walls of the building. Again, a plague of odd events began to manifest. Heiner's foreman was nonplussed when he realized that even after his young aide had tightly screwed a plug into the wall, the plug would pop out of the socket. One plug was seen to follow

Heiner, doglike, as he made his way through a basement passageway.

When Bender arrived on the scene he and his colleagues placed two hooks on a concrete wall and securely fastened each of the screws. Heiner then, under full observation, stepped close to the wall and as Bender watched, the two screws gradually loosened themselves. Heiner's poltergeist soon became more active. Unfortunately, as with Roll in Olive Hill, the boy's parents felt the whole affair to be the devil's idle work with Bender as his arch accomplice.

Investigating a haunted house is much trickier. Hauntings may well carry on for years. Several months may go by with no manifestations and the haunting may even skip certain tenants. Just about the only way one can investigate a haunting properly is to lease the house and pray that it won't be too long before ghostly visitations begin to occur.

Unlike the poltergeist whose concentrated violence has allowed several parapsychologists to witness its displays, the evidence for hauntings often must rest on the combined testimony of the tenants of a particular house. Sometimes this testimony stretches over several years or even generations.

Abbey House in Cambridge is a large house whose main structure dates back to the late sixteenth century. Having had additions twice during the next few centuries, the house is notable enough to be described and listed in *An Inventory of the Historical Monuments in the City of Cambridge*. The well-substantiated haunting of Abbey House, still active today, dates back to the 1860s. The house was occupied later by the celebrated classical scholar J. C. Lawson, who was the first to record systematically the odd events taking place in his home. These records consist of rough notes written by Lawson's wife and an interview with the Lawsons drawn up by Professor F. J. M. Stratton, an ex-president of the SPR.

The Lawsons moved into Abbey House in October 1903 with their two children and servants. During their tenancy two other children were born. It was on the first night in their new home that the Lawsons were introduced to odd sounds and noises. That night, after the household had retired, tremendous bangings pounded the walls. These bangings would center on one door and then be answered on another. The children and maids were terrified, but the Lawsons half-heartedly assured them that the noises were probably caused by the family dog trying to paw its way through a closed door or two.

Soon the bangings changed to footsteps. Lawson recorded: "Heavy footsteps were frequently heard in the next bedroom . . . apparently from the floor of the room above. They seemed unduly loud for a carpeted floor and they were not, so far as it is known, heard by the servants in the room above. . . ." On several occasions, Mr. Lawson, sitting up late downstairs after Mrs. Lawson had retired, would hear footsteps apparently descending the stairs and the rustle of a dress. Though he sometimes went to the door he never managed to see anyone. . . . A Newfoundland dog occasionally seemed to share in the impression, going out apparently to look for someone and coming back disappointed.

The Lawsons were also visited by two phantoms: one of an odd animal, the other of a nun. Mrs. Lawson first recorded the animal phantom in 1904. Their little son John ran out of the nursery crying out in perturbation, "Where's it gone, mummy?" "Where has what gone?" asked Mrs. Lawson. "Why, that little brown thing—it was standing there [pointing to the door] when I came in and it ran to the curtain and it isn't there now."

Most of the Lawson family saw the little animal form as well. Mr. Lawson described it as ". . . a nondescript kind of animal, resembling a large-sized hare, but with close-cropped ears. It was always seen and heard running about on its hind legs, the patter of its footsteps being very distinct and characteristic. It was never seen standing still or moving slowly. Its haunts were the downstairs parts of the house, parts which the 'Nun' never seemed to visit. It was generally seen in twilight but it was also seen quite clearly by artificial light in the drawing room."

The figure of the nun was also seen prolifically once its appearances had been heralded in 1907, three years after the animal phantom. Night after night after the Lawsons retired to their bedchamber, Mr. Lawson would awake to hear heavy, thumping footsteps. Gradually, a form would appear in the room at the foot of the bed, then move away and disappear behind some curtains.

This bedroom seemed to be a particular haunt of this apparition.

Jane Lawson, a child of three years, awoke crying and reported to her mother the next morning that "something came and stared at her—it comes in at the door and comes to her cot and stared and then went and hid in the curtains and she was sure it was a big bear."

Only on one occasion was the figure ever seen outside of this bedroom. The phantom appeared to Mrs. Lawson, ill and in bed, who commanded that the apparition depart. The figure obeyed and was then seen by a nurse in a room across the landing.

In the summer of 1920, G. Granville Sharp, his wife, and daughter moved into the house. In a letter to Professor Stratton, Mrs. Granville Sharp reported further disruption caused by the animal phantom:

> We had been in the old Abbey just a week when I heard, one morning, my little girl Charmian, crying in the hall. I went to see what was the matter and found her in the doorway of the dining room crying hard with the tears rolling down her cheeks. When I asked her what was the matter, she pointed to the far corner of the dining room, by the cupboard, and said, "Will it hurt me?" I answered her that there was nothing to hurt her, but she would not go into the room at any time.
>
> About a week later the same thing happened again—and this time I asked her what it was she saw, and she said it was an "animal" as she called it.
>
> From this time she often spoke of the "animal," and said it came in at the window.
>
> She was only two years and nine months old at this time, and had heard nothing whatever about the subject, nor would she have understood it if it had been mentioned.
>
> I, myself, had heard nothing more than that the house was haunted, until afterwards. And she was always with me, and couldn't have been told of it by anyone else.

Later Charmian apparently saw the nun as well. Mrs. Granville Sharp reported to Stratton that in November 1920 the little girl started talking about a "mummy" that used to come to her at night and peer over her cot.

Both of these phantoms have been reported fairly recently. In 1947 Mrs. Celia Scholfield, a friend of a tenant of the house, wrote to her friend that during a stay at Abbey House her little son,

Christopher, once ran into the kitchen yelling, "Oh look! tiny doggie."

In 1952 Mrs. L. Chimney (a pseudonym) reported a further visit by the "something." Mrs. Chimney arrived at the house in December but did not take warnings that the house was haunted seriously. Having gone to sleep, Mrs. Chimney woke up with the unpleasant sensation of having something shoved into her face. Lifting her hands to her face, she discovered a tray being forced down on her, apparently by the presence of a hand. She pushed the tray aside, got up, lit a light, but found no tray or presence in the room.

In 1955, Professor Stratton himself stayed in Abbey House for a week but did not experience anything unusual. Stratton practiced one of the basic tenets of psychical investigation by residing in the house himself. It had long been known that long tenancy is the only way to insure experiencing a haunting. In that respect when strange stories about the haunting of Ballachin House in Scotland reached the SPR during its infant years, a vice-president of the organization not only leased the house but had several other officials live or at least visit there. Similarly, when Harry Price, the famous British ghost hunter, decided upon a full-scale investigation of Borley Rectory in Great Britain, he leased the house and rounded up a "psychic task force" to live in the old building.

My own experiences in a mildly haunted house came rather by accident. This, too, is not odd, for several psychical researchers have quite by chance stumbled onto hauntings. My colleague, Raymond Bayless, had this good fortune while living in a little house (now pulled down) in West Los Angeles and recorded the manifestations in his first book, *The Enigma of the Poltergeist*.

The little house was built in 1927 and an addition was constructed in 1928. Various tenants lived there over the years but Bayless was able to trace odd occurrences back only to 1953 when the occupant was a Mrs. Jean Mather. In that same year, Ceil Smith and his family, close friends of Bayless, moved in for two years. Bayless himself took over tenancy from 1955 to 1962, the year in which the house was pulled down to make way for an apartment building.

Bayless and his wife began experiencing odd events in the house in 1959, and investigated the history of the house. The owner, Mrs. Smith, confirmed that Mrs. Mather had indeed been disturbed by odd noises and had even called the West Los Angeles police about footsteps creeping about the house and porch which she thought was a burglar. The police could find no one.

Ceil Smith reported that the night after a friend of his had committed suicide he was lying in bed and heard a loud thump in the house. Afterward a scurry of raps of different intensities bombarded the residence. Smith also heard footsteps during the outbreak.

When Bayless moved into the house he did not have any unusual experiences at first. However, several months later when the investigator was reading in the living room, he heard three rhythmic, heavy blows from the back bedroom wall. Later, after Bayless and his wife, Marjorie, retired, a succession of odd raps plagued the little house. Several of these tappings emanated from a drawing board which Bayless used for painting.

In December 1958 Bayless was awakened at 3:05 A.M. by a loud rap. Gradually more raps occurred, at first separated by long periods, then becoming more steady and frequent. The raps, which sounded like someone hitting the walls, took on a metallic quality: "Soon I heard clear, metallic blows, or raps, and I assumed that a long, metal lamp that stood near the drawing board and a stainless steel cover to a tropical fishtank across the room were being struck repeatedly. I actually feared that the tank would be smashed, so loud were the blows. The sounds plainly originated from all sides of the room, and I realized that it was utterly impossible for any conceivable, normal cause to have created the strange disturbance. . . ."

About a half hour after the initiation of these bizarre sounds Bayless heard shuffling sounds also. By this time he had awakened his wife, whose immediate impression was that someone was trying to break in. This paralleled Mrs. Mather's experience.

In 1959 Marjorie Bayless, alone in the house, was to experience a further parallel to Mrs. Mather's encounter. On January 26, Mrs. Bayless was in bed when she heard footsteps on the front porch. Naturally she thought her husband was coming home. Strangely though, Mrs. Bayless did not subsequently hear the familiar sound of the door being unlocked. Getting up to investigate, she found no one.

The next year brought fresh and even more curious enigmas. The first of these occurred on February 3. Bayless was resting in bed when at 10:30 A.M. he suddenly heard a series of faint, high-pitched whistles. The sounds were random and arbitrary, with no pattern or melody. The following day, Ceil Smith, the former tenant, reported to Bayless that he also had heard four high-pitched squeaky whistles. Smith timed this manifestation at between 10:20 and 11:00 o'clock. A most amazing coincidence!

In May 1960 Marjorie Bayless was to be quite rudely awakened by a tactile experience. She awoke with a cry, reporting that something had jumped onto her chest. Later that year she once again heard phantom sounds from apparently outside the house: "I was waiting for my husband to return home when I heard a fast drumming, or rapping, like a tapping on a window pane, or on a hollow spot in the wall, in the frontroom, seemingly on the window, or front door. I said, 'Just a minute,' and went directly to the front door and peered out the window pane in the door. Nothing was to be seen. I switched on the porch light—no one was to be seen—and at that time my husband came around the corner about fifty feet away. He had his arms loaded with groceries and this event took place at 7:15 P.M."

Bayless himself heard a humanlike grunt which startled him from his bed after he had retired. This sound ended the haunting and nothing was further recorded from that time in May 1961 to the final destruction of the house.

When one thinks of haunting one often associates it with houses, abbeys, castles, or crumbling buildings. One would hardly associate it with a large midwestern university. Yet one such campus has been the focal point of a rather interesting haunting.

Mrs. Coleen Baterbaugh of Lincoln, Nebraska, underwent a phantasmal experience at, of all places, Nebraska Wesleyan University, where she did secretarial work for Dean Sam Dahl. On October 3, 1963 she was asked to run an errand which necessitated her walking over to a nearby building. Whisking through the noisy building she was suddenly stopped in her tracks by an intense musty odor as she entered one of the rooms:

> As I walked into the room everything was quite normal. About four steps into the room was when the strong odor hit me. When I say strong

odor, I mean the kind that simply stops you in your tracks and almost chokes you. I was looking down at the floor, as one often does when walking, and as soon as that odor stopped me I felt that there was someone in the room with me. It was then that I was aware that there were no noises out in the hall. Everything was deathly quiet. I looked up and something drew my eyes to the cabinet along the wall in the next room. I looked up and there she was. She had her back to me, reaching up into one of the shelves of the cabinet with her right hand, and standing perfectly still. She wasn't at all aware of my presence. While I was watching her she never moved. She was not transparent and yet I knew she wasn't real. While I was looking at her she just faded away—not parts of her body one at a time, but her whole body all at once.

Up until the time she faded away I was not aware of anyone else being in the suite of rooms, but just about the time of her fading out I felt as though I still was not alone. To my left was a desk and I had a feeling there was a man sitting at that desk. I turned around and saw no one, but I still felt his presence. When that feeling of his presence left I have no idea, because it was then, when I looked out the window behind the desk, that I got frightened and left the room. I am not sure whether I ran or walked out of the room. . . . When I looked out that window there wasn't one modern thing out there. The street (Madison Street) which is less than a half block away from the building wasn't even there and neither was the new Willard House. That was when I *realized that these people were not in my time, but that I was back in their time*. . . .

Mrs. Baterbaugh fled to the hall where she was once more greeted by the familiar and welcome sounds of the students talking and music students arduously practicing. This experience is a rather rare one and is technically called "retrocognition." Retrocognition is an experience in which the perceiver envisions scenes of past events. The experience is so vivid that some people even feel that they have "gone back in time." Actually though, the experience is probably a unique form of haunting. Any one of our five senses may be the recipient of a psychic impression. In retrocognition it would appear that *all* the senses are simultaneously affected by some field of influence that has captured the sound and actions of a bygone day. In these cases the percipient instead of watching an apparitional drama actually becomes part of it.

Mrs. Baterbaugh reported her experience to Dean Dahl and the story was passed around the staff. Someone suggested that the figure by the cabinet may have represented a former music teacher at the school, Clarissa U. Mills. Miss Mills had died in 1936 in a room in the same building that had so affected Mrs. Baterbaugh.

This is how the case rested until 1966 when it was first published. It was quite by accident that seven years later I would come across new evidence that this building at Nebraska Wesleyan University was still haunted and that Mrs. Baterbaugh's experience was not just an isolated incident.

In July 1973 I flew to Durham, North Carolina, to act as a visiting research consultant for the Psychical Research Foundation. The reason for my visit was to work with a phenomenal subject, Blue Harary, a Duke University student who has the ability to induce the out-of-the-body experience at will. Blue was being researched by the Foundation at the time and was engaged not only as a subject but also as a co-experimenter on the work. Since Blue and I were both living in one of the Foundation's buildings we spent considerable time together beyond the scope of our experiments. (These experiments were highly successful and there is no doubt in my mind or in that of others who have worked with Blue that he does indeed have the uncanny ability to liberate his mind from his body. One morning I awoke to see an odd red orb floating quickly through my room. I made a note of the incident and the time. Several hours later I found out that Blue had had an OOB experience spontaneously at that same time and that he had tried to appear to me. Other workers at PRF have reported darting shadows and flashing lights which seemed to herald Blue's OOB presence.)

It was during our casual talks that Blue told me that he had spent his freshman year at Nebraska Wesleyan University and that he had had an unusual psychic encounter there. He told me that the site of Mrs. Baterbaugh's experience had quite a reputation for being haunted. Another part of the building houses an auditorium which because of the building's age was no longer in use. However, Blue knew of Mrs. Baterbaugh's experience, which had been published before he had entered college. In the spirit of a true psychical researcher Blue decided to do a little investigating of his own. His inquiries led him to connive his way into the auditorium and stay there for the night. From here I will let Blue tell his own story of the haunting:

In early 1972 I was independently investigating paranormal phenomena reported to have occurred in the C. C. White memorial classroom building of Nebraska Wesleyan University in Lincoln. Although it was not usually possible to enter the building at night without a key, since the University had carefully locked all of the windows and padlocked the doors, I was able to convince the guard, whom I had come to know during my several months' involvement with the haunting, to let me go into the building alone after hours.

In order to gain entrance to the building one night, I had to phone the guard at his off-campus home. I had unwittingly aroused the elderly gentleman from sleep but he was kind enough to return to the campus and let me into the building at about 10:00 P.M. I thanked him and he left for home once more as I walked into the building and carefully locked the door behind me.

Being careful not to disturb the physical premises, I slowly walked through the halls and passageways with a flashlight and explored the few rooms that had been left unlocked in the nearly century-old building. I was feeling only mild anxiety and was otherwise fairly calm and perhaps skeptical of experiencing anything paranormal that evening.

At about two A.M. I began to settle in the auditorium on the second floor. I sat with my feet over the edge of the stage and made verbal notes into the shoulder-strap tape recorder which I carried with me. I was located roughly in the center of the building. I noted on the tape how my tour had so far been uneventful paranormally. I had repeatedly visited that area of the building where the original phenomena had occurred several years before. I was experiencing the sort of interest which I might feel in a museum; but nothing which could be termed ''psychical'' in nature.

To the rear of the room where I sat were two doors, one on each side of the auditorium, under the balcony. Each of the doors led to a small hallway which had several adjoining rooms and a stairway which led down to both ends of the hallway on the floor below.

I shut off the recorder and shortly began to notice the sound of footsteps coming up the hallway at the foot of one of the staircases and then up the stairs themselves. My immediate thoughts were that the guard had come back to check on how my stay in the building was going. I waited until I heard the footsteps come into the hallway just outside of the rear stage-right door. When they did, I shined the flashlight and called out my location. There was no reply. In a few moments the footsteps seemed to stop just short of the rear entrance and I called out once more quite clearly. My voice seemed to echo and still there was no reply. I wondered why the guard did not seem to be answering me and why he was apparently standing still in the hallway right outside the auditorium. Puzzled, I got down off the stage quickly and went to investigate. In a moment I was in the hallway and found no one there and no one in any of the adjoining rooms. I thought it strange that I had heard no one leave, especially since the elderly guard, if it was him, would have had to run up the hallway and down the staircase in perfect silence to have eluded me; a feat that would have not only been useless, but practically impossible as well, even for an athlete.

Since, on many occasions, I had tried to find someone else who could let me into the C. C. White building at night so that it would not be necessary for me to disturb or worry the guard, I knew fairly definitely that he had the only available key. Additionally, the guard never let the key, which he carried on a belt chain in his pocket, out of his sight. His job depended upon it. At the time, entrance to the building was simply not possible without a key (as I had learned from personal experience) since the University was extremely efficient in its efforts to keep vandals out of the soon to be condemned building which contained many possibly valuable "artifacts" which might be worth salvaging. I am sure that I was completely without the company of other human beings that evening as a result of the security precautions and because of my several uneventful extensive tours of the rooms and hallways during the night.

Yet, the definite sound of the footsteps had been unmistakable. Whatever had produced their obvious arrival up the stairs and into the hallway did not produce any complementary sounds of subsequent departure even though such a departure would have had to have been quite immediate and therefore quite noisy to have eluded me; for even when walking painstakingly slowly in the C. C. White building, it was difficult not to make a sound.

The footsteps had followed a definite, logical, ordered sequence up until their termination. In quality and in pattern the sequence was very unlike the usual creaking of floorboards and settling of almost hundred-year-old wood which I was familiar with there. No, none of these conventional explanations could adequately explain the occurrence of the sound of footsteps coming up the stairs and the non-occurrence of their departure, both of which I consider to be equal oddities. My attitude prior to the occurrence of the phenomena was one of healthy skepticism; not expectant waiting. Since I have never, either before or after that time, had similar auditory experiences either on that evening or on any of other evenings which I spent in the building, it is unlikely that I was the subject of a simple hallucination. The phenomenon was quite discrete; both spatially and temporally and was, I am convinced, paranormal.

Had this been my only unusual experience that night there would have been sufficient evidence of psychical phenomena, especially in light of a previous investigation, connected with the C. C. White building. Yet a subsequent occurrence later that same evening was even more convincing to me personally than that.

At about 4:30 A.M., after taking another tour of the building, I returned to the auditorium stage once more and, using my coat as a pillow, lay down on a large, comfortable bench which I had set up on which to sleep. I became relaxed and settled once more and allowed my thoughts to drift. Despite the incident with the footsteps I still felt only mild anxiety. As I was near the edge of sleep, in what seemed like a split-second, the atmosphere suddenly underwent a drastic metamorphosis.

It was as if a wave of extremely intense energy had come rushing down from the stage-left side of the balcony and engulfed me in its full force. I feel that I shall probably never be able adequately to describe the experience in words. Yet, where I had only moments before been lying in the relaxation of near sleep, I was now suddenly sitting upright and wide awake staring in awe at the rotting, darkened balcony above me.

Experientially, as the wave of energy seemed to increase in area and intensity, I began to feel the White building as an immense mind which surrounded me and which was somehow suddenly awakening. I felt like an unwelcome intruder to a hidden world, as if from all sides the building was staring at me. It was as if I was being told that something was about to occur which I was *not* to witness. Indeed, it was as if the building was acutely aware of my presence and had been tolerating it but that now, when some mystery was about to be manifested, I was not to be allowed to participate. Through all levels of my being I felt a sensation of the Unknown. Deep in the mind of a building that seemed to have become a living organism some guarded secret of the unknown universe was about to be expressed and I was being asked to leave.

Regardless of the consequences though, I decided to remain in the C. C. White building until dawn broke through its dusty windows. I focused strength and mentally expressed my refusal to be frightened from the premises. For a moment, a feeling of tense mental confrontation seemed to permeate the atmosphere. Then the building seemed to deepen its concentration and focus itself solely upon my undesired presence. The walls seemed to be silently shouting that my refusals were intolerable and echoing a command that I depart immediately. Within moments of having been relaxed and nearly asleep, I had begun to experience the loneliest form of naked fear of the Unknown which I have ever felt.

It was a pure fear, a feeling of having no control over what might occur in the next unpredictable moment of my existence. I felt suddenly helpless in the midst of an onslaught whose very dimensions were indefinite. I tossed the recorder onto my shoulder, picked up my coat and slowly but definitely walked toward the rear door of the auditorium, grasping the flashlight, one of the few grips on reality left to me, in my hand. But the flashlight, which had been becoming weaker during the evening, then stopped functioning altogether. I felt chills trembling through my back and chest and leaped down the rear staircase in total darkness. I searched around desperately for the railing and ran down the lower part of the staircase. Once out of the auditorium and on the main floor of the building I felt only slightly more at ease. I ran to the nearest door and forced it open. A welcome rush of cold air greeted my sweating face as I plunged down the cement staircase outside and onto the ground. I stared up as the door slammed shut behind me. The building seemed to have a personality. I got up and kept running until I was out of sight of the place.

Some distance from the building, I began to calm down. It was five A.M. I caught my breath and regained my composure. Now the building seemed distant and unreal. Exhausted, I slowly began walking at a safe distance past the White building and toward home.

The next day I questioned the guard casually about his having returned to the building that evening. His surprise was evident as he replied that he had gone home immediately after leaving me and had spent the remainder of the evening with his wife. He had been very tired and added that he thought he saw enough of the C. C. White building when he was working not to feel the need to return to it when he rather felt like sleeping. I have no doubts about the veracity of his testimony, especially in view of the other facts. He later told me that he himself had unusual experiences when checking the building alone at night.

In subsequent interviewing of others who had experiences in the C. C. White building, the phrase "the building had a personality," and reports of an inability to remain there, even in the company of others, kept recurring.

As an additional note, the night before I was to bring the cassette tape recordings which I had made in the building to a friend at the ASPR the tapes were virtually destroyed in the machine. This has never happened to cassettes in that machine at any other time.

In the last chapter the poltergeist investigations of W. G. Roll of the Psychical Research Foundation were discussed. The PRF is one of the few full-time organizations studying parapsychological phenomena in the United States and is specifically endowed to study those phenomena which would indicate that man survives death. One of the Foundation's major concerns is on-the-spot investigations of alleged hauntings. Several such cases have been reported by the PRF and represent a wide variety of hauntings.

During the summer of 1967 two families, the Franks and the Rubys, reported that their apartment building in Norfolk, Virginia, was haunted. The building was an eight-unit apartment house and the Franks lived directly above the Rubys. The Franks were the main witnesses. They reported furniture shifting about, sounds of crying, footsteps, and knockings. The Rubys reported "cold spots" in their apartment, odd rattling sounds in their kitchen, and the telekinetic movement of kitchen utensils. Jack Kestner, a reporter for Norfolk's *Ledger-Star,* phoned Roll, who sent John Stump to investigate. Stump's investigation included the use of a tape recorder, camera, and three thermistors to judge any shift in temperature. Stump and his fellow investigators stayed two nights on the scene. No actual change of temperature could be measured at the "cold spots" Mrs. Ruby had experienced, nor were any odd sounds or PK witnessed during the daytime investigations. However, nighttime brought some peculiar phenomena. On the first occasion, while all adults were in the downstairs apartment, the investigators distinctly heard sounds as if furniture was being shifted about in the upstairs apartment which could not be attributed to the children there. (Just why not is not stated in the report.) These sounds were repeated on the second night as well and were tape-recorded.

Several days later Stump revisited the house with Dr. John Artley, a Duke University professor of electrical engineering. Again the sounds were heard but they were not as loud nor as noticeable.

Some inexplicable happenings were reported to the PRF by Mrs. Chen (a pseudonym) concerning her Philadelphia house. This old three-story dwelling was the residence of Mrs. Chen, her mother, five children, and a boarder. The haunting was first noticed soon after they moved into the house in June 1967. The chief investigator of this case was Dr. William Joines, also a professor of electrical engineering from Duke University. When Joines went to Philadelphia to look into the matter the residents at that time were Mrs. Chen and two daughters, Mary (twenty-one) and Lisa (twenty-two), a teen-age son, and an infant daughter.

The older daughters were the chief witnesses and had seen an apparition and heard mysterious footsteps; and a few objects had been allegedly moved by some invisible invader. Lisa had been lying in bed one morning when she heard footsteps on the staircase. She caught a glimpse of the figure and since she could not recognize who it was she screamed. No one else saw the figure.

At about the same time Lisa had another experience. She would be awakened in bed by suddenly having the bedcovers pulled off. On one of these occasions she saw an apparition by her bed. She got a good look at the phantom: It was a man with blond thick hair and very prominent ears. Again the girl screamed and her sister Mary ran into the room and also saw the figure. But, as she ran at the phantom it dissipated and she ran right through him. From that time on the figure was seen on several other occasions. Both girls as well as their mother shared in another adventure. Lisa spotted a plastic orange rotating by itself in a bowl of artificial fruit and she called to her sister and mother who also watched the orange's odd antics. This bowl of fruit was the focus of attention during Joines's investigation and served as the only possible paranormal manifestation he witnessed: "On the evening of August 17, the visitors [investigators] and the family were sitting around the kitchen table in the hope that there would be an occurrence. The ashtray and the fruit bowl, which had been involved previously, were placed on the table. After some time a clump of artificial fruit rolled out of the bowl. The family attributed this to a normal cause. However, there is some uncertainty about this conclusion, because the writer had previously stacked the fruit to prevent it from rolling out of its own accord and had then shaken the bowl to check whether the pieces of fruit were firmly lodged. He was the last to touch the bowl and there were no perceptible breezes or vibrations in the room at the time of the incident."

This is certainly not a very striking piece of evidence and the investigation had to remain rather inconclusive.

Joines had better luck with a haunting he and John Artley investigated in northern Florida on behalf of the PRF. The house was the residence of a retired sea captain called Mr. Cole in the report. The house was reported to be haunted with such reports dating back to 1946. However, Cole had not himself encountered anything out of the ordinary until the day he saw two phantoms. These and other phantoms had been seen repeatedly by various visitors to the house, and Cole kept a log of the sightings. All told, about one hundred people had seen odd forms in the house, and their testimony matched that of Cole. Joines was able to interview five of the individuals named in the log and get independent corroboration of Cole's diary.

Joines and Artley visited the house in December 1968 and took along with them the British psychic Douglas Johnson. It was hoped that he could report impressions which would tally with the reports of previous guests. Some of these impressions were rather stock and might well apply to any haunted house. But others were more specific. Johnson described a crying teen-ager. A number of other witnesses had independently described a similar figure. He also described a gray-haired lady wearing an old-fashioned shawl and associated with this phantom the initial M. This description was similar to that of a lady Cole had once known whose last name was Murphy. However, there was little evidence that this impression related to anything haunting the house.

Once while alone in one of the rooms Johnson reported hearing voices and breathing sounds. He also saw a mass of light in a corner of the same room. This latter incident did have some outside corroboration. Coincidentally, Joines had slept in this room during his first visit to the house and, waking up one night, he saw a similar light in the corner. Johnson reported seeing two patches of brownish light in another room which coincided with a similar experience of Artley's in the same room. Donna Cohen, another representative from PRF serving as Johnson's escort, heard sounds of furniture being moved about in a distant room.

Bringing in psychics to help diagnose a haunted house has often been done. Years ago the French physician Dr. Eugene Osty, who subsequently devoted the rest of his life to the study of psychical research, suggested that a number of psychics be introduced into a haunted house to see if their impressions would match one another or the testimony of the tenants.

One of the most tightly controlled experiments along these lines has been conducted by Dr. Gertrude Schmeidler, a New York psychologist. A friend of Dr. Schmeidler's casually remarked to her that she thought her home was infested. When Dr. Schmeidler expressed interest the story unraveled. For the last two and a half years the woman and other members of her family had been conscious of an invisible presence attached to the house. She never saw the intruder but was certain something was there. These feelings were associated only with certain locations in the house. She had never heard any sounds indicative of a haunting but did have the subjective impression that the force was a benign but anxious middle-aged man. The feelings of this presence often became so acute that the woman once ran out of the house during a fit of anxiety over the unseen invader.

A teen-age daughter living in the house also reported similar impressions. Her feelings were focused on the same specific locations as were her mother's. However, in addition, she did think that she had seen something on the stairs of the house. A teen-age son also shared these feelings but the husband seemed to be immune. The mother was prone to attribute these shared experiences with her daughter to telepathy (good old-fashioned suggestion could have done the trick!) but the son's added corroboration coerced his mother into ascribing her feelings to something more than just a subjective impression.

Schmeidler felt the case worthy of investigation. She had a floor plan of the house drafted and had each of the three percipients mark on their copy an X where they felt the presence to be specifically strong. Marks were also made in other areas where fleeting impressions of the presence had been felt. The floor plan was divided into over three hundred units. Blank plans were given to various psychics who visited the house to try to locate the ghost. At the conclusion of the experiment nine psychics turned in floor plans of the house, each marked as to where the focus of the infestation was felt to be. These floor plans were compared to each other and to those marked by the occupants of the house. The results were suggestive. Two of the sensitives agreed fairly accurately with one another and with the family. However, several of them had marked an area in the cellar which the family had not marked. This may easily have been due to suggestion also. A dingy cellar might very well conjure up such impressions in the imagination of a psychic surveying the house.

The psychics were also asked to describe the personality of the presence by checking off applicable adjectives from a lengthy list of possible character traits. Four of the sensitives had similar feelings about the presence which correlated with the impressions of the family.

Unfortunately, this type of experiment really did not verify the haunting. Even Dr. Schmeidler herself had to admit that although the house might have been haunted, ESP from the family or between the psychics was just as plausible. As she concluded in her discussion, "The question of what the family and the sensitives were responding to is still open."

It could well be, though, that these sensitives were actually responding to some sort of invisible animation at the locales suggested by the family. Dr. Schmeidler suggested that her friend might have herself projected "something" which grew into an independent psychic complex existing physically in space which the sensitives could discern. Although she was speaking completely theoretically, some recent evidence might bear this out or at least help us to understand how a haunting might be engendered.

This evidence was uncovered by Graham Watkins who was, until recently, a research associate of the Foundation for Research on the Nature of Man. In conjunction with his wife, Graham Watkins masterminded some striking experiments which seem to illustrate some sort of PK-ESP-healing force. The results of these experiments have considerable implications for parapsychology as a whole and specifically hauntings. He wanted to see if a subject could mentally will a target mouse to awaken before a control mouse. To insure that his results were valid he found mice which were equally sensitive to anesthetics. Two mice would be anesthetized and the subject would then concentrate on waking one mouse first. As he expected, not everyone could succeed in this task, but particularly good psychics were able to perform astronomically above chance.

This alone would merit being classified as a breakthrough since it appeared that ESP could be not only a means of reception, but also of projection. However, Watkins found another pattern that was even more staggering, which he called the "linger effect." He found that the target mouse had to be consistently on either the right or left side of the control mouse. If the subjects had to wake the right mouse and then the left mouse randomly back and forth during the trials with pairs of different mice each time, they got no results. However, if the subjects concentrated on only one side during a whole series of trials with several pairs of mice, success was achieved. The implication of the experiment is obvious—somehow the subject was not only using ESP to wake the mice, but was actually building up a force field which seemed localized in physical space. For the mouse to awaken it must be placed within the spatial field engendered by the psychic. If, for example, the subject focused attention on the right side for a lengthy period of time, and then was asked to shift his attention to the left, the "right-handed" mice would still consistently wake up. Further evidence that some sort of field was being built up came when Watkins placed unexposed film near the target mouse area. This film sometimes showed that it had been exposed. Something had affected it—something more complex than mere ESP.

In the light of Watkins's discovery of the "linger effect," cases such as Dr. Schmeidler's might have a ready solution. Perhaps it really was the tenant herself who was able to create a psychic vortex discernible to a sensitive who came into its presence. It is also not hard to believe that this vortex could become completely independent of its creator and survive his death. Watkins's work also might explain why hauntings often gradually dissipate with time. This vortex would probably slowly die away with time also.

Another of Watkins's discoveries might bear on how hauntings come into existence. As stated, it was found that only a few subjects could wake the anesthetized mice. Watkins took these gifted subjects, most of whom also exhibited substantial ESP ability during more conventional testing, and hooked them up to various apparatuses to determine their heartbeat, respiration, and so forth. Graham Watkins gradually found that certain psychophysiological states were concomitant to a success with waking the mice. This state, typified by an accelerated heartbeat, among other responses, could easily be developed by anyone trained in biofeedback. Biofeedback is a new frontier in psychology which indicates that if a person can be made aware of his own autonomic responses, such as heartbeat, brain waves, and galvanic skin responses, he can then learn to control them through mere will. Watkins took some previously unsuccessful subjects, trained them by biofeedback to enter the state his gifted subjects were achieving, and then retested them with the mice. Lo and behold, they suddenly became successful. So it does appear that this force is generated by the subject being in a certain state of arousal. Perhaps hauntings, which are often linked to tragedy, death, or great emotional upheaval, are produced by an agent who has accidentally slipped into that psychophysiological state which can set up the force field. The field, in turn, generates a haunting. Graham Watkins's work is the beginning of a potential breakthrough.

NINE

further phantoms

Exploring the world of phantoms is much like any scientific expedition: data is collected and classified; discoveries are made; and problems enunciated. In this book several classes of phantoms have been listed. There are phantoms of the living and phantoms of the dead; recognized ghosts and unrecognized ghosts; phantoms that glisten and shimmer and those that are shadowy or invisible. By no means is our taxonomy complete, for there are myriad types of phantoms in the world of the psychic—a world where anomaly is more the rule than consistency.

Throughout this book one point has been emphasized. Anyone might see a phantom. So far we have recounted the experiences of psychologists, writers, housewives, clergymen, even psychiatrists. But if there is one group of people who seem peculiarly gifted in having phantasmal experiences it would be the dying. It has long been known that the dying often report peculiar visionary and apparitional experiences. For far too long such experiences were dismissed as due to either the degenerative action of illness itself, or to drugs administered to the dying to ease their pain and suffering. Psychical researchers are notoriously anti-establishment and instead of routinely accepting these bland explanations they delved into the investigation of deathbed visions to see if perhaps these experiences could be linked to the paranormal.

One such investigator was James Hyslop, whose career in parapsychology has already been spoken of in this book. The other pioneer in the study of deathbed experiences was Sir William Barrett. Barrett was a pioneer in the study of psychical phenomena and in conjunction with various Spiritualist leaders paved the way for the founding of the SPR. Both Barrett and Hyslop actively collected, analyzed, and investigated cases of visions seen by the dying.

A typical example of a deathbed vision is that of the famous tenor James Moore. After his death, the experiences he had were recorded by his personal physician Dr. Wilson. Moore died in the early morning hours with Wilson at his bedside. He was uttering a few words of appreciation to his doctor when suddenly all pathos left his weary face and he entered a state of inexplicable exaltation, crying, "There is mother! Why mother, have you come here to see me! No, no, I'm coming to see you. Just wait, mother, I am almost over. I can jump it. Wait, mother." Moore died soon after.

Such experiences as these are not rare. Unfortunately, though, they are not really evidence of anything paranormal. After all, a dying person might well expect to see welcoming figures and many illnesses affect the brain or cause delirium. Also, many drugs used to ease the suffering of the dying could cause hallucinations or visionary experiences. Clearly, in themselves, such reports as that of James Moore are not very strong evidence for the existence of phantoms.

It was William Barrett who rediscovered a recurring pattern in these experiences. In some cases the dying reported that they saw apparitions of the dead, representing people they could not have known were dead by any normal means. Obviously some sort of ESP or supernormal presence must be invoked to explain these oddities. One such experience was sent to the SPR by J. A. Macdonald, who investigated several such cases and submitted them to that organization.

In the following case Macdonald himself took down all the original testimony from Harriet H. Ogle, who was present at the death of her brother, John Ogle. Part of her statement reads: "About an hour before he expired he saw his brother—who had died about sixteen years before—and John, looking up with fixed interest, said, 'Joe! Joe!' and immediately after exclaimed with ardent surprise, 'George Hanley!' My mother, who had come from Melbourne, a distance of about forty miles, where George Hanley resided, was astonished at this, and said, 'How strange he should see George Hanley; he died only ten days ago.' Then turning to my sister-in-law, she asked if anybody had told John of George Hanley's death; she said, 'No one.' My mother was the *only* person present who was aware of the fact. I was present and witnessed this.''

It would be hard to decide whether this was a phantom or telepathy, even though the dying man apparently did ''see'' a phantom. In some cases absolutely no one present was aware of the death of those seen as phantoms by the dying. René Warcollier was one of the great French leaders in the experimental study of extrasensory perception. Despite the fact that practically all of his contributions to parapsychology were devoted to experimental work he recorded a case of a peculiar deathbed vision in his own family. Warcollier's uncle and his family had journeyed to America but the elder man contracted yellow fever in Venezuela. During his death throes he called out a number of names of individuals he saw in his delirium. Later, on their return to France, the family discovered that these names represented recently deceased friends, announcements of whose deaths were waiting in their unopened stack of piled-up mail. No one present at the death knew of these recent demises.

No hard-core statistics were gathered about visions of the dying until 1961 when Karlis Osis, at that time head of the Parapsychology Foundation's division of research, prepared a monograph, *Deathbed Observations by Physicians and Nurses,* on his investigations. Osis sent out questionnaires to thousands of doctors and nurses to ascertain if they had encountered experiences similar to those collected by Hyslop and Barrett. Unfortunately Osis's monograph catalogued no anecdotes, but did present some important statistics. First, he discovered that his correspondents reported many cases of visions seen by the dying. Further, these visions could not be attributed to the nature of the illness or to any drug sedating the dying. In most cases the phantoms represented figures of close friends or relatives who were already dead and which were seen close to the time of the viewers' own deaths.

While there do not seem to be any predictable rules about who might see a phantom, so far the phantoms recorded in this volume all seem to have common characteristics. They were mostly humanlike or were felt to be humanlike in stature or intelligence. This however is not necessarily true for apparitions in general, for just as apparitions of humans have been chronicled over the years, so too have animal and quasi-animal forms been seen. Like their human counterparts animal apparitions might be crisis apparitions, haunting phantoms, recognizable or unrecognizable figures. In fact, animal apparitions are analogous to human apparitions in a number of ways—they often are seen collectively, at times of accident or crisis, and sometimes show awareness and purpose, and even postmortem apparitions of animals, especially pets, are recorded.

My own favorite case of an animal crisis case, perhaps because a potentially tragic case had such a happy ending, is recorded in *Phantasms of the Living.* In this case, a phantom was not seen but only heard. Mrs. Beauchamp and her husband owned a little mongrel inappropriately named Megatherium (the name of a statuesque sloth). One night they both awakened to hear the pattering of the little pet's footsteps in their room. The couple got up, lit a candle, and looked for the dog. They could not find him and noted in surprise that the door to their room was closed. A short time later, the mystery unresolved, the Beauchamps were disturbed a second time. This time it was by their young daughter pounding on their door crying that the little dog was dying. The family soon found their adored pet entangled and strangling in its neckstrap. Happily, the dog was disengaged and recovered from the ordeal. Could this have been a case of clairvoyance or telepathy? Why then did *both* Beauchamps hear the phantom footsteps?

Unfortunately, not all animal apparition cases have such a harmless denouement. The following is another case of a crisis apparition. Mrs. Marie C. Demler owned a beloved dog named Mac. Expecting a child, Mrs. Demler left the dog with friends before entering the hospital. Several days after, lying in bed recovering from the birth, Mrs. Demler saw Mac enter her room, walk up to her bed, and nuzzle his nose into her outstretched hand. He whimpered for a second and then disappeared. It was learned later on that the dog had drowned at the same time its apparition had appeared to its devoted mistress.

While several cases of crisis apparitions are recorded concerning animals, post-mortem phantoms are also part of the spectral world. As with human phantoms these appear spontaneously, are recognized as representing once-living animals, usually pets, and are often seen collectively, as in the following case reported by Mrs. B. J. Green (a pseudonym) and followed up by the SPR.

Mrs. Green was the proud owner of a pure-bred Persian cat named Smokey. The beautiful animal was lamed in an attack by a dog and finally died from the injury. The cat was buried by the gardener, but this was not to be the end of the beloved pet. Several days later, as Mrs. Green records, "My sister and I were at breakfast and I was reading a letter aloud to her. I was sitting with my back to the window, which was on my sister's left. Suddenly I saw her looking absolutely scared, and gazing out of the window, I said, 'What is the matter?' and she replied, 'There's Smokey walking across the grass!' We both rushed to the window and saw Smokey, looking very ill, her coat rough and staring, and walking lamely across the grass in front of the window, three or four yards from it. My sister called her, and she took no notice, she ran out after her, calling her. I remained at the window, and saw the cat turn down a path leading to the end of the garden. My sister ran after her, calling her, but to her surprise, Smokey did not turn nor take any notice and she lost sight of her among the shrubs."

The phantom was seen continually throughout the day. Only moments after this event Mrs. Green and a friend saw the animal in front of a hedge. The next to see the apparition was a servant. Again the phantom was so lifelike that the servant rushed to give the animal some milk but the phantom disappeared. Finally, the gardener had to dig up the remains to prove that the animal was really dead—for all those who saw it insisted that there must have been some error about the cat's death.

Sometimes post-mortem animal apparitions are so consistently seen that they represent a bona-fide haunting. Such is the case reported by Helen Daniels to the ASPR about a strange adventure she and her daughter shared in 1926.

The family, consisting of Mrs. Daniels, her two children, and nurse, had just arrived in England from the Orient and rented an island house off the British coast from Mrs. Daniels's godmother. The second night in the house Mrs. Daniels's two-year-old daughter, Betty, shortly after having been put to bed, screamed, and running to the child, Mrs. Daniels and the nurse were told that a big dog had come into the room and approached her crib. Terrified, the little girl had screamed. Assuring Betty that it was only a bad dream, the adults checked the house for any animals but, as the reader might have expected, found none.

The very next night, the peaceful house was again disturbed by Betty's terrified screams. Again the girl claimed a big dog had been in her room. Several days later Mrs. Daniels reported the strange incidents to her godmother, who was very interested in what Betty had seen and talked to the little girl. Betty could only say that she saw "a big dog, a very big dog" and that it was black. Mrs. Daniels was told by her godmother that the former owner of the island had a huge black great Dane which had had the run of the island. The dog had been mysteriously bludgeoned to death and its phantom had been seen repeatedly. In fact, several years later, a maid working at the house was also to see the awesome specter.

With these few illustrations of animal phantoms we must leave this fascinating realm of the psychical. A complete discussion of animal apparitions can be found in Raymond Bayless's *Animal Ghosts,* which details many more cases.

Can one make a phantom appear? To answer this question one must be acquainted with a little of the history of parapsychology. Most of the cases presented in this book are spontaneous cases collected by the various organizations for the study of psychical phenomena in the United States and England. It has been argued that the founders of psychical research—Frederic Myers, Edmund Gurney, Professor Sidgwick, and others—were hardly unbiased scholars, but in fact men desperately struggling to find evidence of man's spiritual nature. Instead of studying psychical phenomena dispassionately, they wanted to prove it. To a great extent this was true. It was Myers's hope, for example, that the study of psychical phenomena would clear up many mysteries about man's nature. Myers, Sidgwick, and their colleagues were philosophers and it was with these questions in mind that they embarked on the studies that would occupy the rest of their lives. However, I cannot emphasize enough that these facts do not in any way discredit the painstaking research they conducted, discoveries they made, or the cogency of their arguments. It was perhaps this philosophical seeking which resulted in the extraordinarily tight standards of evidence, critical investigation, and cautious sanctions of individual cases of the paranormal upon which they rested their beliefs about the existence of psychical occurrences. This level of caution and exactitude has become standard procedure in parapsychology and is typified by some recent remarks made by Dr. D. J. West. Dr. West began his scientific career in psychical research which he left to enter other areas of psychology. At a recent conference on parapsychology he commented on how amazing it was to him that science in general has such lower standards and criteria of evidence than psychical research.

Because of this approach the early British and American researchers were not very interested in experimental studies of psychical phenomena. To be sure, such research was being carried out by a few pioneers such as Frank Podmore and Oliver Lodge, but the most important area of research was the collecting of spontaneous psychic experiences of everyday people. When controlled experimentation was instituted by these early pioneers it was directed mostly to gifted psychic subjects, such as mediums, who claimed the ability to receive extrasensory impressions from the dead. The early investigators of parapsychology were philosophically oriented and the fact that human "immortality" could be studied scientifically became their chief concern. This book has reflected the type of psychical research that engulfed the Anglo-Saxon parapsychologists in their quest to collect, categorize, and analyze spontaneous incidents and especially those that bore on the nature of the human personality and the possibility of its survival of death.

Psychical research in continental Europe, however, was surrounded by a very different aura. Just as in England researchers were more philosophically oriented, the European parapsychologists were more biologically oriented. Just as the British were primarily interested in the mind of man, the French and German investigators were more interested in the physical organism of man. Thus, instead of the philosophical minds of Myers and Sidgwick, French and German researches evolved such minds as Dr. Gustave Geley, who saw psychical research as contributing a new dimension to the mysteries of human physiology; the Nobel-prize-winning physiologist Charles Richet, who studied psychical phenomena to discover new powers latent in the human organism; and the Baron Albert von Schrenck-Notzing, a pioneer in the study of hypnosis and sexual pathology, who felt that psychical phenomena critically altered our concepts of human biology.

These men were not so much concerned with man's survival of death. They were more concerned with the discovery that certain persons possessed the ability to move objects without touching them. In the United States this led to the laboratory study of psychokinesis and a new interest in the poltergeist. However, the French, Polish, German, and Italian parapsychologists were fascinated by several gifted subjects in whose presence objects would move, tables would levitate, and phantasmal forms would appear. These researchers such as Schrenck-Notzing and his colleagues were just as cautious and critical as their British confreres, they set themselves the task of answering different questions: Does man have a power that can move objects at a distance? Can this power be controlled? Could it be made visible? Could it be measured? The answers to these questions have a substantial bearing on the subject of phantoms.

There were several great physical mediums in Europe at the time these men were conducting their experiments. Usually a typical séance would go as follows: The medium's hands would be held and the lights lowered or extinguished. Soon the observers might feel odd breezes or "touches." Objects might fly around the room and a table around which they were seated might rise into the air. Often lights or luminous shapes would invade the locked room. When the lights were turned on, the medium would be found still bound or held.

One of the most gifted of these "physical" mediums was a Polish man of letters, Franek Kluski. He was not a professional medium but a brilliant writer and intellectual. All through his life he was prone to psychical experiences and in 1920 he offered himself to Professor Geley and the Institut Métapsychique for rigorous scientific testing. During these experiments the "force" that was the root of Kluski's ability took solid form—phantom limbs materialized, brilliant lights ignited in the air, luminous forms glided through the séance room, and phantoms materialized and were photographed. One might say that Kluski had the ability to create experimentally a poltergeist in a sealed room for experimental study.

It is well known that this type of display can be easily faked since séances are usually held in the dark, and chicanery has always been the scourge of psychical researchers. One must be not only a psychical researcher but an expert magician as well. However, Kluski was never exposed nor was there ever any suggestion that his abilities were anything but genuine. Part of his fame comes from experiments, conducted by Geley and Richet, to obtain molds of phantom limbs seen during his darkened séances at the Institut. During these experiments a bowl of paraffin wax was introduced into the room. The lights would be put out, Kluski would enter trance (a condition of partial or full unconsciousness), and soon a "presence" or force would be felt in the room which would touch the sitters, pull at them, move objects, all while the medium sat immobile, his hands held by the experimenters. The researchers requested the "entity" to dip its hands into the wax, then into a pan of cold water, thus creating a paraffin mold of anything that was let loose during the sitting.

The results of these experiments were remarkable. Humanlike hands of all shapes were formed—right, left, miniature, etc. Often the aperture at the wrist was so narrow, no "normal" hand could possibly have been removed through it without breaking the mold. Further, the sides of these molds were so thin that they could not have been artificially created since gloves made in this fashion are much thicker. It was also impossible that gloves could have been secreted in the séance room since dyes were often introduced into the paraffin at the last moment, as in the following experiment reported by Geley:

> Control was perfect—right hand held by Professor Richet and left by Count Polocki. The controllers keep repeating, "I am holding the right hand" or "I am holding the left hand." After fifteen or twenty minutes splashing was audible in the tank, and the hands operating, covered with warm paraffin. Professor Richet and I had added some blue coloring matter to the paraffin, which then had a bluish tinge. This was done secretly, to be an absolute proof that the moulds were made on the spot and not brought readymade into the laboratory by Franek or any other

> person and passed off on us by legerdemain. The operation lasted as before, from one to two minutes. Two admirable moulds resulted, of right and left hands of the size of the hands of children five to seven years old. They were of bluish wax, the same colour as that in the tanks.

One can imagine the excitement of these tests—an otherwise normal middle-aged man held hard and fast while invisible or luminous disembodied hands flew about the séance room. To this day there has been no adequate explanation to fully account for how these paraffin gloves could have been made normally. And the forces that made them were hands, for even the wrinkles of the skin were reproduced on the molds.

Not only could phantom limbs be observed during experiments with Kluski but phantom forms as well would materialize right in the room with the experimenters. One investigator who had an opportunity to observe this was an American college professor, F. W. Pawlowski, who had several sittings with Kluski in the 1920s and who repeatedly saw complete apparitions created in the séance room:

> . . . the apparitions appear almost unexpectedly beside or behind the medium. In this case I have seen something like a faintly luminous smoke or mist accumulating above the medium's head like a small cloud. The cloud shifts sideways and in a few seconds evolves a human head; or it extends vertically and evolves a complete human apparition, which immediately begins to walk around etc. Very frequently, however, the apparitions appear far from the medium, behind the backs of the more distant sitters, and sometimes in a distant part of the room. . . . The most striking and interesting thing about the apparitions to me . . . was their perfectly human behavior. They conducted themselves as callers at any party. They made a round of the sitters, smiling an acknowledgment of the familiar sitters and looking curiously at the sitters they had not seen before.

These phantoms were photographed. During one experiment by the Polish Society of Psychical Research in Warsaw, tests were run using photographic equipment to try to catch the odd phenomena that broke loose when Kluski was in trance. On December 25, 1919 a sitting was held and after fifteen minutes odd sounds were heard. A photograph was immediately taken and developed on the spot.

An example of one of the Kluski "hand moulds."

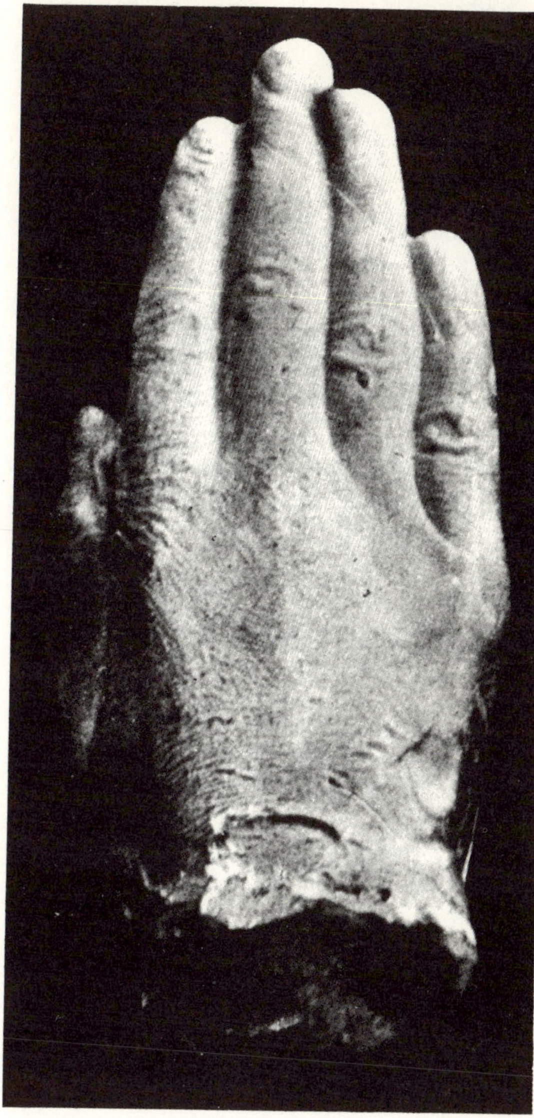

A materialized phantom photographed during a controlled experiment with the psychic, Franek Kluski. Warsaw, December 25, 1919.

There, as a permanent record to Kluski's abilities, was a clear picture of Kluski held by the experimenters with an odd, almost transparent, humanlike figure by his side. Several other photographs were also taken revealing these mannikinlike phantoms.

If one accepts the evidence for the poltergeist, then one can hardly be skeptical of physical mediumship. The poltergeist seems to be a product of one person who uses psychokinesis to act out hostilities. What if this power were more controllable or exercised almost at will? This seems to be the case with those rare individuals, such as Kluski, who were tested time and time again by European parapsychologists under tightly controlled conditions.

Another medium who produced similar phenomena was Eusapia Palladino. Palladino was a semi-literate Italian peasant who more than any other medium of her day convinced psychical researchers that hidden in the morass of fraud and delusion there was a core of genuine phenomena such as telekinesis, levitation, and materialization which occurred in the darkened séance rooms of the physical mediums.

Palladino was discovered by an Italian spiritualist and an early supporter challenged the famed criminologist Cesare Lombroso to test her. Lombroso had the good fortune to witness levitations of small objects while the medium was securely controlled. Lombroso announced his conversion and the scientific community clamored to study her. A commission including Charles Richet was set up in Milan and it also witnessed the paranormal movements of objects and subsequently sanctioned her as genuine.

Several further commissions were held, one in Naples, another in St. Petersburg, and again Palladino's phenomena startled and puzzled the savants who tested her. The SPR in London finally brought her to England but chaos ensued. Although the British experimenters had been warned that Palladino would fake the effects if her hands were not controlled, the SPR experimenters encouraged her to fake. She did and the SPR automatically condemned her as a fraud and her supporters as dupes. However, work went on with Palladino with the more able continental researchers and finally in 1908 the SPR appointed a new commission consisting of Hereward Carrington, Everard Fielding, and William Baggally to test her. All three traveled to Italy to reevaluate the Italian enigma. All three men were experts in the art of mediumistic fraud and expected to expose Palladino once and for all. Setting up an experimental séance room in a Milan hotel, the three men kept tight controls but still witnessed levitations, telekinesis, and partial materializations. They came back to England firmly convinced of Palladino's genuineness.

After these sittings Palladino's abilities began to wane and after another fiasco when Carrington brought her to New York she faded from the parapsychological scene.

During Palladino's early years materializations were often seen during her sittings. Sometimes these would be only "artificial" limbs but in other cases quite human phantoms would materialize. For example, Dr. Joseph Venzano attended a sitting with Palladino at the home of M. Berisso. The medium sat outside a curtained enclosure called a cabinet. "Eusapia became nervous and excited," wrote Berisso. "Suddenly the right side of the curtain swelled out and partly covered the forearm of the medium, which was controlled by Dr. Venzano. Shortly afterwards my wife, Dr. Venzano and I distinctly saw a hand and an arm covered by a dark sleeve issue from the front and upper part of the right shoulder of the medium. This arm, making its way above the free end of the side of the curtain which was on the table, seized [a] glass and carried it to Eusapia's mouth. . . . After that the arm replaced the glass on the table and we saw it withdraw rapidly and disappear. . . ."

These phantom limbs were observed by Venzano at other séances as well. During one sitting Palladino sat with her hands lying in full view of the sitters. Suddenly two phantom hands emerged from the enclosed cabinet behind her and grabbed the medium's head and pulled it back into the cabinet, the medium screaming all the while. On a further occasion Venzano saw the outline of the phantom in full light: "as soon as the white electric light had been lit there was seen advancing toward M. Vassallo [one of the sitters] . . . a human form enveloped in the curtain of the cabinet, which embraced him, while a hand, also covered by the curtain, seized that of M. Vassallo and held it for some time. The medium remained all the time motionless on the chair, her hands in contact with those of the controllers."

Not only were phantom hands and indistinguishable forms seen, but entire phantoms would be built up from the force liberated by the medium. On some occasions these phantoms would represent persons who had died. Venzano was a witness to this as well. At a sitting held on June 16, 1901 several phantom hands materialized and stroked the sitters. Finally these hands grabbed Venzano's and pulled them toward him:

> When my hand, guided by another hand, and lifted upward, met the materialized form, I had immediately the impression of touching a broad forehead, on the upper part of which was a quantity of rather long, thick, and very fine hair. Then, as my hand was gradually led upward, it came in contact with a slightly aquiline nose, and, lower still, with mustaches and a chin with a peaked beard. From the chin, the hand was then raised somewhat, until, coming in front of the open mouth, it was gently pushed forward, and my forefinger, still directed by the guiding hand, entered the cavity of the mouth, where it was caused to rub against the margin of the upper dental arch, which, toward the right extremity, was wanting in four molar teeth.
>
> It should be mentioned that when my hand came in contact successively with the lock of hair on the forehead, the nose, and the chin with the pointed beard, the other hand which guided it pressed upon it and caused it to stop at each with manifest purpose, as though each of these points represented a special sign. I must note, also, that on comparing the indications obtained with those typical of a person who was very dear to me, I did not remember whether the four molars were absent on the right or left side, and that later, after making special inquiries in the family, I was able to ascertain that this defect exactly corresponded with the conditions presented by the materialized form.

The "person" was in fact a relative of Venzano's who had died some time before. Cesare Lombroso also had a similar experience with a phantom that represented his deceased mother. Sometimes these experimentally produced phantoms would even speak a few words, often in dialects unknown to Palladino.

So, to our question, "Can one make a phantom appear?," the answer must be yes. Several great mediums besides Palladino and Kluski had this ability also, although it is a rare one. Yet these experiments were carried out with so much caution and by so many different investigators with similar results that it does appear possible that the human organism has the ability to generate not only mind over matter, but also, as Geley and Richet so ardently insisted, some unknown psychic-biological force that can issue from the organism and mold itself, or be molded, into the shapes of phantoms which can momentarily exist independent of the mediums. Perhaps this is the PK force made visible or, as in some poltergeist cases, represents some form of out-of-the-body experience by the medium. Until more great mediums such as Kluski and Palladino appear on the parapsychological scene, where a new technology can be employed to study them, the nature of this force must remain a mystery.

TEN

the phantom within

Several times in this book the phenomenon of out-of-the-body travel has been mentioned. Many people have had the sensation of being outside their own bodies, often being able to see their own physical bodies elsewhere, travel over great distances, or see themselves draped in an apparitional body. This phenomenon has been recorded in all cultures and in all eras and the reports of it have a general unanimity about them.

So far in this volume several persons have narrated their encounters with the out-of-the-body experience: Colonel Burton was dying when he suddenly found he had popped out of his physical shell; Mrs. Larsen and Mrs. Gladys Leonard had the experience while napping; and Mrs. Landau attempted to appear to her husband in the out-of-body state. It has long been known that apparitions of the living are just as common as apparitions of the dead. The experiments of S. H. Beard are in no way novel and several cases could be quoted. It is also important to note that apparitions of the living are in no way different in their characteristics than apparitions of the dead. This amazing discovery was demonstrated by Hornell Hart who, aside from being a professor of sociology at Duke University, had a lifelong interest in the psychical. His special interest was apparitions and the controversy over survival of death. It was Hart's contention that all evidence pertaining to apparitions should be reevaluated, and this he did in cooperation with several collaborators. The results became his masterpiece, "Six Theories about Apparitions."

In his study Hart compared the characteristics of five sets of apparitional cases: (1) apparitions of those who had been dead more than twelve hours; (2) apparitions of those who had been dead under twelve hours; (3) apparitions seen at the moment of death; (4) apparitions of the living carrying back memory; and (5) apparitions of the living with no memory. These cases were then given an evidentiality rating based on the written or oral testimony, confirmation of the situation leading to the apparition, follow-up investigations, documentation, and time lapse between the occurrence and the record of the case.

After assuring himself that all the cases he used in his analysis were highly evidential, Hart mapped out the characteristics of the five apparitional groups and discovered that they all shared the same features. From this data he verified his three base hypotheses: apparitions may be ESP projections of living agents (out-of-the-body experiences); apparitions of the dead are indistinguishable from apparitions of the living; apparitions carry motivation.

What does all this mean? It has long been believed that man has a superphysical "soul-body." When this vehicle is liberated the out-of-the-body experience occurs. Further, on rare occasion, this vehicle might be seen as an apparition. Far from being telepathically created pictures, it can be argued that out-of-the-body experiences and apparitions of the living actually represent the manifestation of a psychic body that dwells within each of us.

What has led to this belief? First, there is the testimony of hundreds upon hundreds of people who have had the experience. Some of the occurrences have already been recorded in these pages. There are many others. One famous case is that of L. J. Bertrand.

Bertrand was a clergyman who had a passion for mountaineering. On one occasion he and some of his students were climbing in the Alps. Not being able to keep up with his youthful companions, he decided to let the team move on without him and he gave the guide orders about the tracks to use and the position the students were to maintain on the ropes. The company left and Bertrand decided to light up a cigar. To his horror he discovered that he was numb with cold and that his whole body was freezing from the icy air that swept across the mountains. There was nothing he could do as he sat there, the paralyzing cold creeping over his body. Suddenly he discovered that he was no longer in the body, that he was floating above it connected by an "elastic string" extending between his physical and superphysical bodies. The out-of-the-body state enabled him to see that his guide had not only entirely disobeyed his orders, but was nibbling on Bertrand's lunch and sneaking sips from the bottle of wine which he had brought along. Later on Bertrand had a vision of his wife.

Unlike many stories of phantoms, this one had a happy ending. Bertrand, just as suddenly as he had left, found himself reentering his body. His guide had found him half frozen and had revived him. Although the guide had saved his life, Bertrand rather ungraciously accused him of stealing his meal and disregarding his directions. The guide was, as the report goes, justifiably perplexed.

Other out-of-the-body experiences are even more vivid and the projectors describe themselves as being enveloped in a new apparitional body. Mr. F. Thompson writes:

> I was lying on my back. Eventually I heard a droning sound. The noise became louder and louder when suddenly I found myself no longer in my bedroom but seemed to be standing on a high plateau overlooking a beautiful countryside. The scene vanished. I then felt myself falling through dark space and I prayed. Immediately I found myself in my bedroom, fully conscious and apparently hovering horizontally over my body! This hovering "body" of mine seemed like a diaphanous composition, and its form seemed to be a counterpart of my physical self and aligned above it correspondingly. I seemed to be only a few feet above it and, after a short space of time, slowly sank down into it. I then heard a rushing noise and a large "click" in my left ear, immediately after which I felt fully integrated with my physical self. Not once . . . did I lose my sense of being in a state of complete consciousness.

Experiences such as these have led many to believe that man possesses an ultraphysical body. Critics have argued, though, that it would be hard to separate these cases from hallucinations accompanied, in certain instances, by ESP. Is there any solid evidence that man possesses a phantom?

The one man who has done more than anyone else in tackling this problem is Dr. Robert Crookall. Dr. Crookall began his career as a geologist specializing in fossil plants. His list of scientific achievements would insure the bona fide of any scientist. Holding both a Ph.D. and D.Sc., Crookall was on the faculty of the University of Aberdeen before becoming the principal geologist of the H. M. Geological Survey. His scientific publications include several books on geology, including a four-part proceedings on fossil plants. But in spite of the great achievements Crookall retired from geology to pursue another endeavor, the study of the out-of-the-body experience, which had engaged his interest long before his first published book on the subject in 1961. Since then he has written over a dozen books concerning the out-of-the-body experience and the evidence that the phenomenon does indicate the existence of an ultraphysical phantom that is locked within each of us and projects during the out-of-the-body experience.

Crookall's data and opinions are based on close to one thousand narratives that he has culled from the literature of psychical research as well as from firsthand accounts. From these accounts Crookall has constructed four different lines of evidence that the out-of-the-body experience could not be a hallucination.

Crookall's first line of evidence is that out-of-the-body narratives follow general patterns and have indicative characteristics. These traits are hard to explain as being caused by hallucination or any other type of pathology known to psychiatry. The percipient feels that he is leaving the body through the head; a blackout then occurs; the apparitional body is seen to hover above the physical body; this posture is resumed before reintegration; a blackout then occurs once more; rapid reentry causes shock to the physical body. This is not to say that all out-of-the-body experiences have these characteristics, but they do crop up so often that they are considered general peculiarities of the experience.

Dr. Crookall then compared two sets of reports and made further discoveries which constitute his second line of evidence. He separated out-of-the-body experiences occurring normally as during sleep, illness, near death, etc., and compared them to enforced out-of-the-body encounters such as those caused by suffocation, shock, anesthetics, etc. In making this comparison he found that the two sets of data while outwardly resembling each other had significant differences. For example, enforced out-of-the-body excursions were much less vivid than natural ones. These differences were so statistically significant that they were way beyond a million to one odds of having been only a freak. This feature, too, is hard to explain away as being caused by hallucination especially since superficially the traits appear to be identical until closer inspection.

Crookall made this same type of comparison between the experiences recorded by famous psychics and mediums and the reports of hundreds of everyday people who reported the experience. Again he found characteristic differences between the two sets of data. Psychic individuals had less vivid experiences than did normal people, much the same as the differences between enforced and natural experiences. This was the third line of evidence.

The last line of evidence concerns the mechanics of the experience. Again, by analyzing his reports, Crookall discovered that many projectors reported what seemed to be a two-stage release of the apparitional body while others reported a one-stage release. In going over his data in light of this discovery, he found that a general characteristic of these experiences is, in fact, a two-stage release. First the individual appears to leave his body and is immersed in a confused, misty environment. This unclouds as the apparitional body more clearly releases from the physical body. This is then reversed at the end of the experience. One-stage releases are also reported. This type of "mechanics" is unlike any hallucination.

Crookall's data is very compelling and although I have heard many people argue that the out-of-the-body experience is a hallucination which may use ESP, I have never met any one of these critics who could successfully counter Crookall's data—much less explain all of his data along other lines. In short, Robert Crookall's data is more than just suggestive that man possesses an ultraphysical soul-body.

Who then has the ability to project this phantom? It seems that the general situation which causes the experience is more important than the personality. Just about anyone might have the experience. What is more important is the consideration, if man does have a phantom within, can he voluntarily control it? If so, this would destroy the hallucination theory since one cannot control or manipulate hallucinations to any extent. Is there a method for inducing the out-of-the-body state? I would now like to analyze these questions and then discuss my own experience of phantoms. However, in this case the phantom was my own! *

Several talented individuals in the history of psychical research have been gifted with the ability habitually to induce the out-of-the-body experience. Most of these persons have recorded their encounters in autobiographies such as Sylvan Muldoon's *The Projection of the Astral Body,* written in conjunction with Hereward Carrington; Oliver Fox's *Astral Projection;* Cora Richmond in her *My Experiments Out-of-the-Body;* and more recently Professor Whiteman in his *The Mystical Life.*

Interestingly, each of these writers has to some extent chronicled methods which he has found helped to induce the out-of-the-body state. Oddly, although these authors differ on some points they do agree on others in the various methods they suggest. The fullest procedures were written by Sylvan Muldoon and Oliver Fox. Fox, whose records were published before Muldoon and Carrington collaborated on their epoch-making book, outlined various courses. He wrote out instructions to the experimenter to relax, be still, and concentrate on each part of the physical body, willing the double to release itself from each successive point of concentration. He then suggested concentrating attention on the top of the skull, trying to reach an imaginary trapdoor. He called it the pineal door. Fox's method, in retrospect, is very significant since Robert Crookall, in analyzing spontaneous cases for his *Study and Practice of Astral Projection* and *More Astral Projections,* reports that a high percentage of persons undergoing the out-of-the-body experience have the sensation of leaving the body *through* the head. Thus Fox's method seems to have been based on good empirical observations.

Sylvan Muldoon was a little less rigid in the suggestions he outlined for inducing the out-of-the-body experience. His book was written in response to a summary of the work of the French pioneer Charles Lancelin, given by Hereward Carrington in his 1919 volume, *Modern Psychical Phenomena.* Charles Lancelin wrote (in 1913) a huge volume of over five hundred pages on astral projection entitled *Méthode de dédoublement personnel,* which, lamen-

* The following material is greatly expanded from an article of mine which originally appeared in *Fate* magazine.

tably, has never appeared in translation. However, up to that time it was the most complete work ever written on the subject. Lancelin gave rather elaborate conditions under which the "double" could be exteriorized. First of all the right subject must be chosen, preferably one of a nervous temperament, in good health, calm, mentally placid, with an exceedingly strong will. (One might add that to find all these qualities in one person would constitute a phenomenon in itself.) Lancelin proposed that this individual should, before falling asleep, repeat to himself, "I have will—I have energy," or a like phrase. This was to be continued until sleep set in. The next step, on the following day, is almost identical to Fox's method published a year later. Every inch of the body should be concentrated on, the "double" being willed to separate. However, after this ritual all concentration should be focused on the solar plexus, the subject, while breathing deeply, willing an out-of-the-body experience to take place. The subject should imagine himself leaving the body, projecting to a point in space. If these methods are followed, Lancelin wrote, then a projection experience would occur. He also outlined atmospheric conditions which would aid the experience.

Muldoon, having read of Lancelin's work, was not too impressed by it and wrote Carrington that he (Muldoon) had undergone the experience several times and found many discrepancies with Lancelin's report. The rest is history; a correspondence ensued and in 1929 the authors jointly presented *The Projection of the Astral Body,* devoted almost entirely to Muldoon's own experiences. This is perhaps the most famous book ever written on the subject.

Muldoon suggested many varied ways to prompt the out-of-the-body state. One of the methods he proposed was to induce the "double" to carry out a need that the physical organism cannot. Then he proposed that a person wishing to experiment with the out-of-the-body experience should go to sleep thirsty or hungry, which might induce the "double" to be projected. Like Lancelin, Muldoon also stressed the mental state of the subject—his temperament should be cool, emotionally calm. He also suggested that the subject be on his back during the experimentation.

Muldoon's most elaborate method is similar to Fox's and Lancelin's use of willpower. His routine consists of, first, deep breathing.

The next step is, like Fox's, to project all thought to the top of the head and try to tense and relax the scalp muscles, then tense and relax the facial muscles, the neck muscles, the upper arms, down through the entire body, alternately tensing and relaxing. The next step is to relay the thought into the heart until the whole body feels the pulsations of that organ. After this condition is reached the subject must learn to be able to shift attention and become aware of pulsations in any part of the body. After mastering this skill comes the tricky matter of controlling the speed of the heart.

During the actual projection experiment these pulsations must be concentrated upon, and steadied, and slowed. Muldoon believed that this practice, if mastered, would automatically lead to the out-of-the-body state without actual conscious method. This routine is not, like Fox's or Lancelin's, a means of inducing the experience but a manner of placing the body in a state where such an experience may be allowed to take place.

Muldoon proposed other methods also. One procedure was to stare into a mirror, scrutinizing oneself, trying to convince the consciousness that the image in the mirror is the real self and gradually falling asleep during the exercise. He also stressed use of what he termed "the passive will" method—a procedure chiefly devoted to hypnotizing the will into unconsciously wishing to project at a certain time.

All of these methods have some degree of conformity and some unique aspects. However, do they work? Perhaps some people can induce the out-of-the-body state by using them. There is one method, though, that has been tried with success by psychical researchers, and it is this fantastic story to which I would like to turn.

In Muldoon's book some methods are cited which were used with success to produce out-of-the-body experiences by Prescott Hall. The main point of these experiments was a rather odd number of dietary regulations. Muldoon, however, missed the significant fact that these methods were given to Hall through "communications," recorded through the mediumship of Mrs. Keeler, allegedly from the dead, before any of the Lancelin, Muldoon, or Fox reports were ever published or known of. These were published in the *Journal* of the ASPR in 1916. Hall had two friends who claimed the ability of conscious projection. He questioned

Mrs. Keeler's "communicators" about methods to produce the phenomenon in order to test them himself. He was actually testing Mrs. Keeler's mediumship, for he wrote, "Suppose that certain instructions not to be found in published occult writings, if followed by the experimenter, result in certain phenomena. Suppose that other experimenters repeat the processes and arrive at similar results. It would seem that either a medium must have discovered the teaching or that it is supernormally communicated."

In the Keeler data we find the following methods: a method of concentrating the attention on mental images of lights, then imagining the self as a point floating in space. Several images are used to induce the out-of-the-body experience, including the image of swirling out of the body, images of a cone, passing through a waterspout, passing through a hole in one side of a tank, the concentration upon one's image in a mirror. (Muldoon probably took his ideas from this account by Keeler.) Another method is use of breathing techniques, especially those including "holding of the breath."

The phenomenal thing about these communications is that they reveal many techniques hit upon by persons having spontaneous projections. For instance, Crookall, in noting the similarities occurring during the out-of-the-body experience, also records sensations such as swirling, projecting through a cone or to a pinpoint of light—all information given through Mrs. Keeler *before* anything was known about the phenomenon. Crookall was so impressed by the Keeler material that in 1964 he wrote his *The Techniques of Astral Projection* which was devoted to it. For example, Keeler's "communications" noted the "silver cord" extension between the "double" and the physical body, such as the Reverend Bertrand noticed, long before Muldoon reintroduced the observation (thought by many to be the first writings on the cord in English). Mrs. Keeler's controls also told Hall that there were differences in the vividness of natural out-of-the-body experiences and experiences that were artificially coerced. Crookall was to prove this half a century later.

One of the most unique aspects of this very unusual case is a list of dietary regulations which the "communicators" listed as helping to induce the out-of-the-body experience. These said that meat should not be eaten, fruit and vegetables should be concentrated upon, carrots were especially beneficial, as were raw eggs. Nuts were extremely bad but liquids were helpful.

Hall followed these techniques for six years with some success. He recorded his experiences in the *Journal* of the ASPR in 1918, and although he was never greatly impressed by his own partial success, his records show such remarks as "freer from the body than before and able to move through it, especially horizontally." And later, "Sense of physical body falling down and away. Definite feeling that I am not in my body." Still later, "Feeling of being drawn out of the body . . . feeling of being pulled about." Thus it seems that Prescott Hall, by following the Keeler communications, did have some marginal success.

I first came across Hall's writings in 1965 and was intrigued by the dietary regulations. They were easy to follow and were not clouded in vagueness such as "projecting one's mind" or "will control." I was at that period spending quite a lot of time experimenting with different methods in trying to induce the out-of-the-body state, but with little success. I had followed Muldoon's techniques with utter failure even though I had been able to achieve control of my heartbeat.

I had finally decided to give up conscious endeavors to promote an out-of-the-body state but I did institute the dietary regulations Hall had suggested. I must admit that, even here, there was a matter of self-indulgence since I couldn't bear raw eggs and did eat meat, though in lesser amounts than I was accustomed to. I kept to this diet for two weeks and in August 1965 I suddenly underwent a very unexpected out-of-the-body experience one afternoon. While I don't want to dwell on these personal events, it is necessary for me to explain them in order to show how I discovered a method of my own for inducing the experience.

I had arrived home one afternoon feeling so tired that all I wanted to do was to lie down. I turned on the radio and then stretched out on my bed. I fell asleep off and on, and then unexpectedly I had the peculiar sensation of being awake but feeling as if my body were falling swiftly. I didn't quite realize what was happening and turned onto my other side. Then I noticed that my body was rigid and I felt as if it was pulsating and falling. At this time I realized that a projection might be taking place. I was able to flip onto my back and concentrate on the feeling of falling. The next instant I found myself staring at my own body. I turned around; my "double" swayed and fell to one side. I found myself moving toward the door and then, blacking out for an instant, found myself awake, my pulse very slow. I usually have a very fast heartbeat.

A few weeks later the same experience recurred, though this time it was oddly different and much more interesting. I had again decided on having an afternoon nap and shortly thereafter I felt those same pulsating sensations. All at once I found myself crouched on my knees beside my bed facing a cabinet which was perpendicular to it. I realized that an out-of-the-body experience had taken place and my only wish was to try to get out of my bedroom. Immediately I was standing up, moving toward the door. Everything looked hazy, as in my other experience, the entire left side of my face felt crushed in, and my vision was obstructed. I moved toward my closed door, passed through it, and went into the living room. Immediately I found myself awake on the bed again. The significant fact here was that I was sleeping on my left side with my face cushioned on my arm which was exerting some degree of pressure on the left side of my face and also obstructing my sight.

These were the most startling of all my experiments. It is difficult to tell exactly what method had done the trick, so to speak, since I had been trying every method I could find. However, at the time of these experiences I had stopped conscious practices, so the out-of-the-body experiences were due either to self-suggestion, all the factors combined, or the dietary regulations. To this day I don't really know though I favor the explanation that the Keeler method was the prime catalyst.

Feeling that I had demonstrated to myself that a person could induce the experience I stopped experimenting altogether. What I did not realize was that the experiments had somehow affected me psychically and from 1965 to 1968 I was to undergo a great many partial projections, a few experiences which were probably fully out-of-the-body, but more important, I was able to develop a system of my own to induce the OOB state, wholly unlike the methods developed by Muldoon, Fox, or Lancelin. In rereading the Keeler material I find that I should have expected this. Mrs. Keeler's ''communicators'' specifically stated that after initial practice the dietary regulations could be discarded but that the experimenter would continue to have the experiences.

After my two experiences in the summer of 1965 I felt that my experimentation had ended. I no longer followed the prescribed instructions for inducing the out-of-the-body state and had turned my attention to other endeavors. It wasn't for several months that I discovered that somehow I had, by my experimentations, upset that delicate balance which normally keeps the out-of-the-body experience from taking place. The subject had been put out of my mind, but one evening as I was lying in bed, half awake, I became faintly aware of a mild rushing sound in the distance. This background sound grew until I heard it as an overpowering roaring in my ears. I tried to move but found myself cataleptic and falling. By exerting all my energy into moving my hand I was able to stop the experience. (This is a technique recommended by Sylvan Muldoon, who was one of the first to discuss the cataleptic state which may precede or conclude the OOB experience.) At the time it didn't dawn upon me that the experience was an incipient out-of-the-body projection until it was repeated a week later. On that night the same phenomenon occurred, although in this case during the cataleptic state I saw several white faces to the side of me. I must admit that I was so frightened that I stopped the experience and turned on a light for the rest of the night. Although I have studied this field for some years this is the only time I ever felt really frightened!

It was in trying to analyze these experiences that I hit upon a method of inducing a projection. Both Muldoon and Fox wrote on the significance of dreaming and of the hypnagogic images which immediately precede sleep. Fox suggested that one might be able to catalyze the experience by dreaming. Although it is somewhat rare, some individuals have the ability to know they are dreaming when they are in a dream state. Usually this is accomplished by noting incongruities which could not pertain to the ''real world.'' (Recently Celia Green has written a volume, *Lucid Dreams,* devoted to this phenomenon.) It was one of Fox's techniques that once a person is aware he is dreaming he can produce an out-of-the-body experience by willing himself to awaken, and upon waking automatically be in a projected state. This general plan is in keeping with the observations of the Dutch researcher F. Van Eeden, who wrote of a similar phenomenon. What Fox called the "dream of knowledge" Van Eeden termed the "lucid dream." According to Van Eeden, when one is aware he is asleep he can send out his dream body from the physical body, thus producing an out-of-the-body experience. Van Eeden's experiences, one might add, predated Fox by over fifteen years and were published in an early issue of the *Proceedings* of the SPR.

Through this same period I was discovering certain alterations in my own dream states. On several occasions I was able to become aware that I was in a dream state, and although I was able to force myself to awaken—hopefully projected—I was able to reach only a simple cataleptic state with falling sensations. Unfortunately, these techniques led to some confusion since it is not odd for an out-of-the-body experience which takes place during sleep to be mixed with dream symbols. Many of Fox's experiences seem to be infiltrated with his dreams, as were Van Eeden's and Whiteman's.

However, what was so intriguing to me was that so many of these experiences occurred not after I had fallen asleep, to then awaken in a partially projected state, or what Fox calls the false awakening, but occurred before sleep had set in and seemed to be related to the hypnagogic state. Many persons before actually falling asleep fall into a borderline state during which they "dream," but are actually awake. This state, akin to daydreaming, is full of mental pictures and it is during this state of consciousness that many psi experiences seem to occur.

It has long been thought by astral projectors that this state could be used to manipulate the out-of-the-body experience. Muldoon himself suggested that this area of consciousness could be used to develop the knack of projection. However, he never expanded the theme.

It was also during this time that I became aware that my hypnagogic state was very rich in images. Unfortunately these images are hard to study since they are fleeting and any conscious attempt to study them usually leads to a "waking with a start" type of consciousness. However, it was at the time of these incipient out-of-the-body experiences that I began to study my own images and try to prolong them. After a while I was able to extend them for a few seconds before coming either to full consciousness or falling to sleep. It was during these observations that I discovered that my incipient projections were becoming allied to these images. I remember one of my most vivid experiences which related the hypnagogic image to the out-of-the-body experience. I was lying in bed and had the image of driving very fast in an automobile, downhill, and as I reached the bottom of the incline I was jolted into consciousness. However, I found myself fully conscious and could "see," but I was also fully aware that my eyes were closed. I was cataleptic and felt myself falling. I realized that I was in an incipient projection and willed an out-of-the-body experience to take place. For a second I felt a sensation of extreme pressure and then was aware of an instant of great relief. For a few seconds I felt that I was floating above my body. I seemed to float downward and then "woke" into full consciousness.

A week later another similar experience took place. I was taking a Sunday afternoon rest and had begun to fall asleep. I was in a hypnagogic state and had the image that I was driving in my car toward a freeway underpass. I became aware of a feeling of heat as I approached it. This feeling was rather unpleasant so I decided to stop the image and come back to consciousness. To my surprise I found myself paralyzed. It is hard to describe the sensation. I was "dreaming" that I was driving in my car, yet fully aware of being "awake," yet cataleptic and with a feeling of intense heat over my body. As I drove nearer the underpass I grew warmer and warmer until the feeling of heat became almost unbearable. I finally reached the imaginary underpass and the image dissipated, but I found myself still cataleptic with the indicative sensations of leaving the body still manifesting. For about half a minute I struggled to leave the body, getting to the point of experiencing "dual consciousness"—the sensation of being in two bodies at the same time, but unlike my previous experience I was unable to project and popped back into full normal consciousness.

It would seem that my "driving dreams" are similar to the "falling dreams" of many persons. These dreams have never been explained; some psychologists feel the dream is a reaction to the physiology of the conscious entering various levels of sleep. Others find a correlation between falling dreams and sexual symbolism, while astral projectors consider them to be examples of unconscious out-of-the-body experiences. Whatever the cause, over the period of 1965–1968 my own experiences merged with my driving images in the hypnagogic state. It was then that I learned that through the hypnagogic state I could repeatedly produce the experience. And this led to the method I am about to describe.

Fox and Van Eeden both used the dream as a catalyst to coerce the out-of-the-body state by shifting consciousness from a dream state to a projected state. I felt no need actually to enter a sleep stage to accomplish this maneuver. Especially since I was rather bad at producing "lucid dreams," which happened only by accident and not by design.

I was in a hypnagogic state one night when I became aware of the sensation of driving along a narrow road. For some reason I intuitively felt that if I could sustain the image long enough to drive my car off the road and crash it, this would shift me into a projected state. My first attempt was successful. I crashed my mental automobile and found myself fully conscious but paralyzed, with indicative falling sensations. I relaxed and concentrated on these sensations and soon became aware of not being in my body. Then came a blackout and I was back in my body.

My method of controlling the out-of-the-body experience thus culminated from direct control of the hypnagogic images. The actual procedure is rather simple, but the techniques are tricky. One must first of all be aware of one's own hypnagogic state, which one usually is not. Then one must learn to view this state panoramically without aborting it. Finally one must learn to control and prolong the images and use them for one's own purpose. In essence this technique is no different from the general theory behind the methods of Fox or Van Eeden. The important difference lies in the fact that the consciousness never is lost and is never interrupted by the sleep stage. Thus, the pollution of the out-of-the-body experience by dreaming is not such a problem as it seemed, in retrospect, to have been with Fox and Van Eeden.

The key is in discovering what hypnagogic image is related to the out-of-the-body experience and then learning how to stop the image but shift the consciousness into the OOB experience instead of into a waking stage. If one can learn to produce certain hypnagogic images, the procedure is easier. If one can induce an image such as driving, falling, etc., these can be used to induce the out-of-the-body state. The key is that one must find a point where the image comes to a climax. In my own case it was reaching a specific point while driving and to crash the car which prompted the projection. I can cite one experience with the "lucid dream" which ended in a false awakening.

I was in a corridor and saw a large trash chute. I knew that if I jumped through the chute I would have an OOB experience. I jumped in and immediately woke up, I thought. I found myself paralyzed and suddenly floating above my body. My "double" reversed its position and then I blacked out and woke back in my body.

Theoretically I would explain the mechanism this way: since the hypnagogic state is neither a waking nor a sleeping state, by consciously controlling it, one can control the out-of-the-body experience since it seems that at this point the consciousness is least dependent on the physiological mechanisms of the organism. Since many out-of-the-body experiences are reported as occurring on the verge of sleep, by controlling this stage of consciousness one can more ably direct the experience than at any other time.

I could not conclude this chapter without some word of warning. Although I have had these experiences and have used this technique with success, I have rarely discussed them with anyone except a few colleagues. My reason for this is a belief I share with Robert Crookall that conscious experimentation with astral projection is actually dangerous for very basic physiological and psychological reasons. For example, I have mentioned that rhythmic breathing aids in projection. Breathing exercises, especially cross-breathing techniques, can seriously upset one's physiology and put abnormal pressure on the heart. Staring into a mirror can cause dissociation. Conscious control of the heartbeat can backfire and instead of controlling the heart one can actually throw it out of rhythm so that it beats sporadically, too quickly, and completely out of control. (I suffered from this for over a year because of my experimentations.) Other techniques can affect the oxygen supply to the brain. I think these physical dangers are enough to warn away the would-be experimenter.

Why then do I write this? For one thing, as with the self-hypnosis fads of the 1950s, we are now in a period where the craze is for psychic development. Everyone wants to be psychic and this desire leads many people into self-delusions of personal psychic abilities. Today there are a few self-proclaimed "teachers" who profit from the cravings of many and claim to "teach" astral projection despite the danger involved both physically and psychologically. These "teachers" exact high fees for their services, but anyone familiar with the academic literature on the out-of-the-body experience can immediately see that they have most likely never undergone an out-of-the-body experience in their lives. Every field has its con men and parapsychology is no exception. So I have tried in this chapter to present some of the real methods.

My own experiences were very gradual and my attempt to control them was a process which was developed on spontaneous experiences. This does not mean that these experiences have been in any way a revelation, and for every good experience I have had a bad one. For instance, one night I woke up cataleptic and attempted to leave the body. I tried to sit up in bed in my "double." I succeeded and although the room was black, I was aware of dual consciousness—one head reclining on the pillow the another sitting up in bed. I couldn't maintain the state and felt myself falling back into sleep. The next morning I tried to get out of bed and discovered that my abdomen was so racked by pain that I could hardly walk. What caused this peculiar aftereffect? I don't know. On another occasion I became aware of being pulled out of my body by the way of my head (going out through the head is a common experience) and although I wanted to curtail the experience, I found that I could not break the catalepsy and that I was leaving my body against my will. Only by bringing concentration back to consciousness could I end a truly frightening experience. I have outlined a method not for inducing, but controlling the experience since if any scientific work on this state is to be done, the experience must be controlled. My success with this technique comes from my own predisposition to the experience since I still have strong, though fogged, memories of out-of-the-body experiences as a young child. But learning to control the OOB experience is not the same as trying to coerce it. The OOB experience occurs normally during sleep, during times of illness, and near death. It can be forced by suffocation, drowning, a sharp blow, or hypnosis. All the methods outlined for inducing the out-of-the-body experience by Muldoon, Fox, Lancelin, and others generally use a technique which produces the projection by physiological means—self-hypnosis, such as willing the "double" to release, or staring into a mirror, or suffocation (breathing exercises which upset the respiratory system are dangerous procedures).

If one has a history of this fascinating experience by all means cultivate that ability. This can only lead to breakthroughs in our scientific study of the phenomenon. If not, I suggest the would-be experimenter analyze his own motivations for entering into so risky a practice.

What does this all mean? The characteristics of the out-of-the-body experience cannot be explained as being due to hallucination. The fact that one can experimentally induce the state is also a severe argument against the hallucination theory. Finally, the fact that one can experience himself as an apparition at the same time that an observer also perceives the subject as an apparition, as in the Landau experiment, is also suggestive that we all harbor a phantom within.

No one has come up with a satisfactory explanation for what an apparition is. Edmund Gurney felt that apparitions were telepathically created images. This theory might account for some cases, but what of apparitions of the dead seen long after the person's death? Who is the telepathic agent? What of collectively seen phantoms and those who move objects? One parapsychologist told me that an apparition is a subjective hallucination triggered by ESP which uses PK. This explanation is hopelessly burdensome. A better try was an explanation given by F. W. Myers, Gurney's colleague. Myers thought that phantoms were not actually physical but that they did occupy space and created some sort of psychical vortex. Unfortunately, Myers did not explain where and how this enigmatic and contradictory form came from or about. G. N. M. Tyrrell hypothesized that a psychic center was built up from both the agent and receiver, who jointly built up an apparitional drama. This could explain reciprocal apparitions such as the Landau case. However, Tyrrell in the long run was postulating some type of out-of-the-body experience since he felt consciousness might follow and be present within the apparition. But Tyrrell still felt that apparitions were nonphysical, which cannot adequately explain many facts such as why apparitions intercept light or are reflected in mirrors.

This brings us right back to the central problem. What is an apparition? Neither Gurney nor Myers was very aware of the out-of-the-body experience although Myers seems to have once undergone the experience. They knew about it, but no concrete data concerning the phenomenon could possibly have been known until the writings of Muldoon and more importantly Crookall and Hart. The same is true of Tyrrell. Until Crookall's painstaking research there was little attempt at arguing that the out-of-the-body experience was the release of a real ultraphysical body. Occultists had always claimed this but there was no concrete evidence except some very obscure French researches of which few were aware.

Since evidence favors the idea of a human double—and no one has successfully argued against the data that Crookall has assembled—this may well be the solution to the enigma. What one sees as an apparition is a liberated "double." The only serious challenge to this theory made by Hornell Hart was that it could not explain why apparitions are dressed in everyday clothing. However, I have already argued that phantoms are seen by an intermingling of sense perception and psychic perception, and our own minds or the apparition's could easily create the necessary illusion. Those who have had the out-of-the-body experience have also had this experience. They find themselves naked, worry about the odd situation, and instantly find themselves fully clothed! This explanation solves the riddle of apparitions of the living. It can also explain apparitions of the dead, for there is no reason that the double could not survive death after the demise of the physical body. Since the out-of-the-body state represents a temporary release, death might well be a permanent release. This is the opinion of Dr. Robert Crookall, Hornell Hart, and many who have had the experience. This "double" could then appear to the living on occasion. Since the "double" is strangely physical and nonphysical at the same time it can explain many anomalies of apparitions such as the movement of objects, collectivity, and the ability to vanish.

I am sure many readers, students of psychical phenomenon, and other parapsychologists will be wary of this explanation. However it is built solidly on the foundations of the "four lines of evidence" assembled by Crookall and the data he has amassed, as well as being offered in the light of the inadequacy of more conventional theories to explain phantoms. As Crookall himself has stated so explicitly, "Any who reject our hypotheses, which manifestly embrace and explain all the facts, are in honor bound to advance better hypotheses—and show, specifically, and in detail, that they perform that task satisfactorily."

ELEVEN

toward a new reality

Psychical phenomena are one of many "unnatural things" that haunt our earth, our civilization, and our lives. And just as with any foreign or misunderstood stranger, we usually react with fear or apprehension. However, when one surveys all the fortunate, or if the reader prefers unfortunate, individuals who have confronted apparitions, telepathy, and premonitions, the supernatural becomes a little more "natural" to us. The past few decades have seen remarkable scientific achievements and as with the Victorians of Darwin's time, so many today feel that there is no mystery or problem that science cannot tackle or will not ultimately solve. Still, all in all, the processes of the mind remain nature's most guarded secrets. Even with all the studies made in biochemistry, with Freud's masterful insights, and our new understanding of human behavior, the causes of mental illness are still a mystery. Even why we sleep is still an enigma.

Today, thanks to a handful of researchers, ESP, mind over matter, apparitions, and a host of other forbidden topics have become much more familiar to the general public than they were before the second world war. But even though these phenomena are more familiar and accepted this does not mean that they are any better understood. In fact, although we have collected much data on what affects psi, as psychical phenomena is often abbreviated, and what aids it to manifest, the basic process and mechanics of this elusive faculty is still a mystery even though there has been an upsurge of scientific investigation into the psychical.

Just as with anything else, once an unknown quantity becomes familiar to us we stop thinking of it as mysterious. Fifty years ago the idea that one could affect one's own physiological processes such as heartbeat, brain waves, or blood circulation was scoffed at as being "occult nonsense," yet today, biofeedback, which has clearly demonstrated these abilities, has become integrated with mainstream psychology. The same is true of hypnosis, once condemned as a parlor game for charlatans. Many sophisticated people today accept the existence of ESP and other psychical manifestations as a fact of life and even as an important part of their world view. This is perhaps due to the great interest shown in parapsychology by a portion of the scientific establishment and by the way psychical phenomena have been presented and exploited by the mass media. Since we have been bombarded with evidence and information about the psychical, the subject no longer seems as mysterious as it would have only a few decades ago.

Another reason that parapsychology has begun to achieve a niche in our scientific culture is that people are, quite frankly, beginning to realize that the supernormal is quite a natural thing. For example, ESP is not reserved to great psychics, mystics, or visionaries but recorded by normal people in every state of human consciousness. The same goes for phantoms. No level of human consciousness is immune from apparitional experiences. We tend to think in terms of our own mental lives as existing in only two distinct states, sleeping and waking, but there are many other states, as anyone who has experimented with hallucinogenic drugs or who has gone through the strange voyage of madness can tell you. Yet, if apparitions were so unnatural, why would they occur in all of these different states of human consciousness?

By far most of the people whose narratives have been recorded in this book had their experiences while fully awake, that slim segment of mental life with which we are most familiar. Is there really anything *that* unnatural about the following experience of a British woman walking home leisurely from a civic meeting?

Miss Mary Paterson had just turned into a brilliantly lit street in one of England's quaint but busy towns. "I had walked but a few paces when I was staggered by seeing, as in a cinema show, reflected in the air in front of me a clear-cut picture of my brother in Australia, lying with the unmistakably helpless look of a dead or unconscious man who has just fallen. I saw his pose, his clothes, and even his thick curling hair as if in life before me." The vision or phantom soon vanished only to reappear again during her walk. Miss Paterson realized that something must be seriously wrong with her brother and reported the strange visitation to her sister, who rather scoffed at her. Nothing immediate was learned about the odd experience. Only two days before they had received a chatty letter from their brother. The denouement did occur the following day when the sisters received the sad news that their brother had fallen from a ship, had been knocked unconscious, and had died later at a hospital. This was just as Miss Paterson had seen in the vision.

If Edgar Paterson had been found well and alive there certainly *would* be something "unnatural" in Miss Paterson's experience. Not counting optical illusions, normal people do not have unaccountable hallucinations. One might think that perhaps Miss Paterson was "a bit off," or, if this experience were recorded today, that perhaps she was one of so many of today's youth who have experimented with LSD or mescaline and have seen weird hallucinations. But no, Miss Paterson was just another run-of-the-mill human being who in a perfectly normal state saw a vivid hallucination induced by telepathy or clairvoyance. With all the evidence for ESP and other psychical phenomena is it really at all strange that Miss Paterson might, via some form of extrasensory perception, become aware of her brother's injury or that her brother might exercise some unknown faculty to contact his sister? Miss Paterson obviously thought not, for instead of the self-questioning that one goes through after experiencing the paranormal, she apparently accepted her experience at face value without fear or anxiety. She knew what it meant despite the skepticism with which her report was met when she told her sister of it.

Even ten years ago people who had psychical experiences often began to question their own sanity. Brainwashed by a materialistic society that stated such phenomena do not occur, people naturally began to think that perhaps their minds were cracking and off to psychologists and psychiatrists they ran. Unfortunately, it is a sad fact that until only very recently these professionals were in no way qualified to help since they themselves had little working knowledge of parapsychology and probably did more harm than good by giving therapy instead of reassurance as to the naturalness of such experiences. Luckily, today most people accept and even openly discuss any psychical adventures that may befall them. The unknown is becoming much more accepted by our society.

Another quite normal mental activity is sleep, a rather enigmatic state in which we spend a great portion of our lives. Sleep, to many, is an escape from the hassles of day-to-day living. Sleep can also be an escape from pressing emotional problems. But it certainly is not an escape from ESP. In fact, if anything, sleep is more conducive to the psychical than our waking consciousness. A few simple statistics will reveal this: A study made in the United States showed that in spontaneous ESP cases over 50 percent occurred during sleep while only about 35 percent happened during a waking state. Similarly, a study made in Germany revealed a two-to-one ratio of dream ESP to waking ESP in the cases surveyed. A very recent study made in India showed a similar preponderance of dream cases. To my knowledge the only study that did not conform to this pattern was one compiled in Great Britain. Outside of this one study, though, the statistics are staggeringly supportive of the theory that we experience ESP more often during sleep than while awake. Although this is not the place to explain or theorize why this occurs, it probably is related to the fact that in our waking lives we tend to sublimate psi experiences since they cause anxiety. During sleep this natural defense is weakened, thus allowing more ESP to enter into the consciousness.

Just as dreams are normal to sleep, so are phantoms. Dr. George Johnston was visited by a phantom during sleep which he reported to his nephew, who verified the story later. After Johnston had fallen asleep he had a curious "vision." He saw two soldiers wearing khaki uniforms standing by a pile of clothes and accouterments. Johnston intuitively knew that these discarded things belonged to his son, Alec, serving in the military. The two men went through the materials and let fall a pair of muddy boots and Johnston heard them talking about Alec's death. Upon fully waking he reported the dream to his nephew, who shared his amazement. Four days later they received word of Alec's death.

A more obvious phantom, which disturbed the peaceful escape of sleep, was recorded by the SPR though the name of the percipient was kept confidential. Mrs. F., as she was called, had been a house guest of a German baroness who died on April 29, 1930. A notice of the death, which stated only the date of death, was posted to Mrs. F. However, Mrs. F. really didn't need the notification since she already knew of the death: "On the Tuesday evening [of April 29th] I went to bed feeling very tired about 9 P.M. and fell sound to sleep. About 11:15 P.M. I awoke with some-one pressing a kiss on my forehead, and on looking up I saw *the Baroness standing by the side of the bed,* she looked as though she desired to say something, or was waiting for me to speak or answer, but I was so startled, not to say afraid, I was speechless, so after gazing at one another for a minute or two the Baroness vanished. Her expression was so sad and inquiring I cannot forget it. . . ."

Mrs. F. reported the experience to her husband the next day. This was before the official notice of death arrived. Thus, Mrs. F. had a witness to her claim. She fixed the time of her vision at about 11:20 P.M. which was very close to the time of the Baroness's death.

While phantoms seem to appear during normal and sleeping states, psychotics, especially schizophrenics, seem particularly prone to out-of-the-body experiences. Now the first thought that comes to mind in making this claim is naturally, if these people are psychotic, can we rely on their "hallucinations"? It is quite true that psychotics live in a mental world isolated from our "real" world. Theirs is alive with presences very real to them but not to us. However, many psychotic "delusions" may harbor hidden truths. That schizophrenic hallucinations might represent a psi effect so intrigued me that when I was invited to attend the Parapsychology Foundation's 1972 International Parapsychology Conference in Holland, I quickly chose it as the topic of my paper.

At that conference I argued that psychotics may be very sensitive to psi impressions which may complicate their "delusions." I tried to find a perfect case of this, but although there seemed to be none, the anecdotal evidence was impressive. However, my perfect case did materialize (no pun intended) just a few weeks later when I attended the Parapsychological Association Convention in Edinburgh. At that conference a British psychiatrist, James McHarg, reported a rather unusual case of schizophrenia. The patient constantly had the delusion that "Beasts" were living in her ears. Later McHarg discovered that the patient's brother, whom she had not seen or heard from for several years, had developed severe ear infections, the onset and development of which exactly corresponded with the onset and development of the patient's delusions. Obviously, the entire paranoid psychosis was based on ESP impressions from her brother. My perfect case was a bit tardy but no less valuable to me.

It had long been my contention that many delusions of being "without a body" reported by schizophrenics really represented actual out-of-the-body experiences. I was able to demonstrate this by comparing some of these "hallucinations" of typical psychotic or drug-induced body-image distortions to the characteristics of out-of-the-body experiences recorded by normal people. The "psychotic" cases were very similar to the latter and not at all similar to "body-image distortions." So, it seems, even the flight from sanity does not bar one from an experience of phantoms.

Miss Thelmar, for example, was a journalist who under severe emotional pressure had a brief psychotic attack. At its onset she recorded an almost classic out-of-the-body experience which she narrated in her fascinating memoirs, *The Maniac:* "On the bed lay my physical body, fully awake and conscious. Directly over it, at the distance of a few feet up, was poised in mid-air my human soul, consisting of a replica of my physical body made of a substance like flame—" Miss Thelmar felt that her "soul" was separated from both of these bodies. This is not odd. Such cases are reported and I, on one occasion, had an out-of-the-body experience in which I "saw" both my physical body and my double from an independent vantage point. Some of Crookall's cases report this also. Note the horizontal position of the "double" so typical of the out-of-the-body state and not at all like hallucinations.

I do not think it odd that people in these various states of consciousness had experiences of seeing or being a phantom. If anything, research in parapsychology has shown that people in all states of consciousness have psychical experiences. Seeing a phantom is not at all unlike any other extrasensory phenomenon. What we are seeing is some sort of projection from a person—living or dead—that has been released from the confines of the human body. And after all, isn't that what telepathy is? Apparitions are, then, very related to ESP itself. They are "seen" via ESP, and they might be induced by ESP. When man's ESP force coupled with PK "goes out" from the body we might have an apparition. I have suggested that apparitions might be "doubles" seen during out-of-the-body experiences. Could not the "double" itself be a composite of our ESP and PK, the essence of the human personality? All this can get very complex, but the important factor is that psi experiences are so normal to mankind that no level of human consciousness is excluded.

Many people have had dramatic ESP experiences during their normal waking hours. A typical and very famous case is that of Mrs. Bettany, which was included in *Phantasms of the Living*. When the percipient was a child she was walking home reading a book on geometry. Suddenly she had a vision—she saw a bedroom in her home and her mother lying on the floor as though she had expired. The little girl went immediately to a doctor-friend and urged him to follow her home since his aid was necessary. The doctor was understandably nonplussed since the girl admitted not having been home at all. Nonetheless he followed her home to find her mother lying on the floor incapacitated by a heart attack. Mrs. Bettany's psychic vision actually saved her mother's life.

As stated before, statistics on ESP occurrences tend to show that spontaneous cases occur more often during sleep, especially via dreams. The following is a typical dream-ESP incident sent to the Society for Psychical Research: "On the night of the 17th October 1931 I dreamed that a man died on the couch of my sitting-room. I did not recognize him although I saw him very plainly. I related my dream at breakfast to members of my family, which was a Sunday. My father-in-law came to supper that night, and when starting for his home, he was taken ill and we were unable to move him to bed. He died on the couch in my sitting-room on 19th October. . . . It was totally unexpected."

This is a typical case of precognition—ESP of a future event.

Such cases are so very common that a famous British aeronautical engineer, J. W. Dunne, started to record his dreams night by night, hoping to chronologue and verify dreams of future events. This he did with success. On one occasion he dreamed of a violent volcanic eruption which later occurred, and on another he dreamed of being chased by a wild animal in an open field. This too was realized. Dunne recorded so many precognitive dreams that eventually he theorized that these premonitions were in no way psychic at all, but completely natural occurrences if one understood time correctly. He explained his theory about time but I am afraid no one can understand it. As one parapsychologist told me when I questioned him as to whether he could comprehend Dunne's theory, "No, I can't, but I think I know where he made his error!"

Some experimental parapsychologists have taken a cue from these cases and have attempted to see if one could experimentally induce telepathic dreams. It was hoped that the wonderlands of sleep would be more conducive to psi than our normal waking periods. The results have shown promise. These experiments were spearheaded and developed by Montague Ullman, a psychoanalyst, Stanley Krippner, an experimental psychologist, and later by Charles Honorton. All three carried out this work at Simon Maimonides Hospital in the medical center's dream laboratory. In these experiments, which have received wide publicity and attention, one person would stare at a painting in one room while another person was sleeping, monitored by mechanical equipment so that the experimenters would know when a dream state was occurring. Often these dreams would be too similar to the paintings being sent telepathically at the same time to be purely coincidental.

In one experiment the target was Tamayo's painting of two dogs viciously eating a chunk of meat. Meanwhile the percipient dreamt of being annoyed by a guest at a banquet because, "she wasn't very good to invite for dinner because she was very conscious of other people getting more to eat than she, like especially, meat. . . ."

Coincidence or telepathy? All in all, the Maimonides team has run several such tests, many of which had a close semblance between the painting and the dream. Usually though, complex statistical evaluations are made whereby judges give numerical ratings to paintings and dreams and in several studies, although the actual dreams were vague, when scored by the judges the overall statistics were very suggestive of ESP. The judges tried to match dreams with paintings and chose the correct one time and time again. However, what is truly exciting are those few cases where the themes themselves are so obviously associated.

The hypnotic state has an old and very interesting relationship to psychical phenomena and research. The hypnotic state is not totally understood for it is not a waking state nor really a sleeping state. It is just one of the many altered states of consciousness that the mind of man can explore.

When hypnosis was first "discovered" in the eighteenth century by Franz Anton Mesmer, one of the first discoveries made by the early mesmerists, as hypnotists were then called, was that during the mesmeric or hypnotic state, subjects would sometimes become aware of the experimenters' thoughts, other ESP phenomena, distant occurrences actually taking place, or would diagnose the medical problems of others. Several subjects even seemed to become psychic when hypnotized. One of the greatest of these talented subjects in modern times was Madame Morel, who was arduously researched by a French physician, Eugene Osty. On one occasion Osty handed the hypnotized clairvoyant a little book of Esperanto. She described the owner—a tall, lanky young man, a battle in which he fought, his being wounded, and his capture and death. Osty sent a transcript of this reading to the investigator who originally gave him the book, Dr. Emile Boirac. Boirac wrote in reply that Mme. Morel's clairvoyant abilities, which manifested when the subject was hypnotized, had given a correct description of events leading to the death of the owner of the book.

Another famous case of a hypnotically induced ESP experience concerns Charles Richet. Richet's colleague, Pierre Janet, a famous French pioneer in the study of psychology, hypnotically entranced a subject and instructed him to visit Richet's laboratory in Paris which was many miles away, via ESP, and report what he saw. The subject frantically reported a fire. In fact, Richet that day had a terrible fire in his laboratory.

These anecdotes were so commonly reported in the early years of research on hypnotism that the Parapsychology Foundation decided to support a project to collect and evaluate all of those old reports and experiments. The final collection encompassed four volumes and these were published as a set, *Abnormal Hypnotic Phenomena,* edited by E. J. Dingwall.

Meanwhile experimental parapsychologists also became intrigued by these old cases, and in fact, when J. B. Rhine began his epoch-making research at Duke University, this topic of hypnotically induced ESP was one of the first projects he and his associates were interested in evaluating. It was through these experiments that Rhine discovered that several subjects were star ESP performers in a perfectly normal state. The rest is history.

Recently several tests have been run to see if the hypnotic state is especially conducive to ESP. As with all altered states of consciousness ESP is not foreign to the hypnotic state, but is there any special affinity as the anecdotal evidence would imply? Several experiments would suggest that this is so. Jarl Fahler, a Finnish parapsychologist, ran quantitative experiments similar to Rhine's card-guessing tests and found that subjects while hypnotized did much better on the ESP tests than subjects who were not. Lawrence Casler, a New York researcher and psychologist, ran an experiment in which both the senders and receivers were hypnotized and secured high ESP scores. In India, Ramakrishna Rao found that hypnosis was conducive to clairvoyance, and Charles Honorton has run many successful tests on ESP and hypnosis. If one were to compare all the experimental tests carried out using hypnosis as an aid more experiments than not would support the theory that hypnosis does seem conducive to ESP. Again, it appears that the ESP ability is a normal faculty of our minds.

Charles Honorton and Stanley Krippner, along with their dream research, have had a major interest in hypnotically induced ESP. After surveying all the research carried out in this area they concluded, "While many problems of both methodology and interpretive importance remain to be resolved, it would appear that hypnosis provides one of the few presently available techniques for affecting the level of psi test performance." These experiments also show how valuable discoveries can be made about ESP by taking suggestions from spontaneous cases and testing them experimentally.

Waking, sleeping, even hypnosis are states of mental functioning that are familiar to us. Yet, even the more bizarre states of the human mind contain an ESP element. Perhaps no area of altered states of consciousness has aroused the public interest more than the subject of hallucinogenic drugs such as LSD. Psychedelics have been credited with everything from inducing religious experiences to chemical psychosis. So of course, experiments were soon designed to see if these drugs might also induce ESP.

Unfortunately, such experimentation has been extremely limited. Because of the mass media's coverage of the drug epidemic that spread through our culture, tight legal controls were instituted which prohibit most research on LSD. The tragic part is that the irresponsible coverage drugs received in the press caused cancellation of many studies which could have had a profound effect on our knowledge of the processes of the mind.

The experimental evidence that psychedelics can induce ESP is limited and not very compelling. A lengthy project was carried out in Holland testing psilocybin-affected subjects. Standard card tests and psychometry tests were made with no above-average results. In Italy Dr. Emilio Servadio and Roberto Cavanna carried out a series of experiments in which subjects given either psilocybin or LSD gave impressions about the contents of sealed envelopes. Although some of the subjects gave accurate ESP impressions of the pictures concealed in the envelopes, the overall results did not show that the psychedelic state was any more prone to ESP than the normal consciousness.

This is not to say that ESP is totally unknown to the psychedelic state, for as in hypnotically induced ESP there is some anecdotal evidence that ESP may freely manifest during a psychedelic trip. Many travelers and adventurers who ingested psychedelics with primitive tribes in South America have reported ESP experiences. Colonel Morales reported that he took yagé, a strong organic hallucinogen, in Peru. During his "trip" he became aware of his sister's death in Rio de Janeiro. A month later Morales received word of his sister's death, which had occurred about the time that the colonel was experimenting with the drug.

Two experimenters who pioneered research into psychedelic drugs were R. E. L. Masters and Dr. Jean Houston. During the early years of research they recorded hundreds of psychedelic sessions and noted that some ESP experiences were reported: "S-19, a housewife in her mid-thirties, complained in the course of a LSD session that she could 'see' her little daughter in the kitchen of their home and that the little girl was taking advantage of her mother's absence to go looking for the cookie jar. S then further reported that the daughter was standing on a chair and rummaging through the kitchen. She 'saw' the child knock a glass bowl from a shelf and remarked that the bowl had shattered on the floor, spilling sugar all around." Later, on returning home, the subject found that all these events had actually taken place.

Masters and Houston were so struck by many such reports that they carried out some further rough ESP experiments. First they tried standard ESP card tests, and while some subjects scored poorly others did amazingly well. These star subjects when tested without psychedelics did not score as well. Later, the experimenters carried out a more elaborate test where the subject had to describe the scenes written on slips of paper sealed in envelopes. Some interesting results were obtained. For example, when a slip read "a sailboat off a rocky coast" the subject responded with his mental impression of a "sailboat sailing around a cliff."

I have gone on at some length about ESP and where it manifests for one simple reason—to show that psychical experiences are so common that there is no way we can escape them. No matter what state of mind we are in we are never free from the possibility of psychic impressions. The same is true of phantoms. As with ESP they too can startle us when we are awake, disturb our sleep, and as with the subject quoted above who "saw" her daughter, even appear while we are in radically altered states of consciousness. Experiences such as seeing phantoms are really very natural ones.

Most of the cases quoted in this book have been recognized phantoms, phantoms seen at the moment of crisis or death, or figures of deceased friends or relatives. This selection was intentional since if an apparition of a recognized person is seen, recorded, and certified by witnesses before it is learned of the death or injury this is striking evidence for the paranormal. These types of cases have always been stressed because of their veridical nature. After all, psychical research was, and still is to a great extent, on the defensive—so much so that unverified or unwitnessed psychic experiences are of little use when trying to reason with a skeptical scientific community. This might have led the reader to believe that when a phantom is seen it usually is indicative of some special event, such as a death. This is not so. Seeing a phantom is such a common experience that many people have seen these forms spontaneously without recognizing who "they" were or what "they" wanted. One percipient wrote: "I saw a figure standing by my bed. I had been awake for some time. It was a summer morning about 5 o'clock, and I saw the figure quite distinctly. It was tall and dressed in something grey, falling in long folds. The face was kind and I was not frightened at first, but it suddenly changed and the whole figure and face, as it were, fell to pieces in the most ghastly manner and vanished. . . ." The narrator never knew who or what the figure was.

Mr. and Mrs. C. wrote to the SPR how they had seen a weird figure collectively: "My wife and I were both asleep, when I woke suddenly, found her sitting up, also just awake; she said, "What is that?" At once I pointed to where, at the bottom of the bed, I saw distinctly a white figure, unrecognizable, which at once vanished." Again, the reason for the appearance of this strange phantom is ambiguous.

Perhaps this indicates that just as with ESP there are phantoms all about us, just out of reach of our senses.

The fact that we are influenced by a bombardment of impressions that do not always reach the senses leads us to the fact that our concept of reality requires great alteration. Most people would argue that reality is an objective thing and that our world is completely independent of its viewers, such as you and me. While this may be true we must not forget that reality may be quite different to different people. The reality of an aquatic animal would consist of a very different reality than that of a land animal. Certainly, the mystic who transcends into indescribable vistas during states of ecstasy and rapture has a different concept of reality than the common man. The physicist who studies the mechanisms of the universe also sees reality in a different light than a scientific layman.

We experience reality five ways—through seeing, hearing,

touching, smelling, and tasting. Through these senses we experience the outside world. But are we necessarily entitled to assert dogmatically that what we experience is the totality of reality? To us, the fact that radio waves and other electromagnetic waves penetrate our homes allowing us to watch leisurely our television sets or do our garden chores to the accompaniment of a radio announcer enthusiastically covering a Sunday afternoon baseball game are common facts of life. Although we cannot see these waves, we can control them and they are understood by scientists. However, it was only about a hundred years ago that these forces were even discovered, yet they existed all the time even though we had no way of knowing about them or gauging them. What other mysterious forces exist in the universe that we simply are not aware of because as yet we have no way of detecting them? Gamma rays, radiation, *et cetera,* all existed and bombarded our planet long before we knew they were part of the universe.

Could it be that our senses allow us to see only a slim portion of our universe? I am prone to think that our universe transcends what we ourselves experience. True reality must be infinitely more complex. There are several occurrences that cannot fit into our scheme of reality. Take, for instance, Fortean phenomena. The term is named after an eccentric genius, Charles Fort, who collected and classified reports of scientific anomalies. These weird occurrences in nature that have no normal explanation have become a special genre named after him. Can our understanding of reality explain such events as the following:

Strange disappearances. Off the coast of Florida is an area called the Bermuda Triangle, a geographical area into which planes and ships have entered and quite literally disappeared from the face of the earth. No wreckage has ever been found, nor the people involved ever heard from again. Tracers sent in to search for missing ships and planes have in some cases vanished also. These disappearances are still occurring today, and science, though recognizing that the Bermuda Triangle represents a startling anomaly, has no explanation for these utter and total disappearances. Can our common reality explain this?

Strange rainfalls. Instead of rains of water there have been recorded rains of tropical fish, human blood, peas and beans, huge chunks of ice, and other inexplicable things.

Strange footprints. There have been several instances of completely inexplicable footsteps appearing out of nowhere. In England residents of several towns awoke one snowy morning to see cloven footprints marching up the British Coast. These footsteps walked over walls and roofs, through large bodies of water, on and on. An animal perhaps? But in one short night these footsteps marched over one hundred miles! Several other such occurrences have been recorded.

Quite frankly, if our understanding of reality is correct, none of the above events could possibly have happened. Yet they did and still do. There are few scientists today studying these anomalies, although there are several organizations devoted to investigating them.

True reality must take into consideration these uncharted dimensions just as it must take into account the existence of psychical phenomena. Apparitions and kindred phantoms are inexplicable in terms of our common reality but by expanding our concept of our universe to include the fact that forces exist completely beyond our comprehension and that our four dimensions may be only an opening door to many further dimensions, they may become more understandable.

If psychical phenomena radically alter our concept of reality and life, they must also alter our concept of death. Throughout this book I have passed over the natural controversy that apparitions prompt: Do these figures represent the activity of the dead? Does our present view of reality really require us to conclude that man cannot survive death in some new dimension and have an influence on us of this world?

There have been several spontaneous manifestations of apparitions of the dead that are hard to explain as being anything but figures engendered by the personalities of the dead themselves. The famous psychic Mrs. A. W. Verrall had some encounters with phantoms of the dead: " . . . as I was washing my hands in a little room at the end of the passage leading to the front door . . . I heard footsteps, and looking up saw a little old lady coming towards me. She was dressed in a dark dress gathered round the waist in full folds, a grey knitted shawl over her shoulders fastened with a brooch in front and a cap. I did not see her face although she was walking towards me. I knew at once it was a hallucination but was neither startled nor alarmed. The figure disappeared before reaching the room where I was. During the next two or three weeks, I saw 'my old lady,' as I called her, more than once—always facing me, and in the act of approaching. . . ."

Mrs. Verrall saw the phantom several times both in Brighton, where she was visiting, and when she returned to her home in Cambridge. Although never seeing the phantom's face, Mrs. Verrall identified the figure as her great-grandmother, who had been dead for ten years, by the distinctive brooch which had belonged to her and which appeared on the phantom.

What or who was this phantom in actuality? First of all, it could not be merely a hallucination. Normal, healthy people do not repeatedly hallucinate figures. Obviously, the phantom was independent of Mrs. Verrall. The phantom was not a typical ghost since it followed her when she left the residence in Brighton where she first saw it. The apparition appeared dressed, even to jewelry, so we can conclude that the figure was not really objective but more likely a form projected to Mrs. Verrall's ESP by a foreign intelligence. But whose? If Mrs. Verrall projected it she certainly would have created it with a face to identify the phantom conclusively. By process of elimination it seems the only really logical explanation would be that the apparition was a form engendered by or consisting of the post-mortem personality of Mrs. Verrall's relative. If this form had appeared at the time of the old woman's death one could rightly argue that Mrs. Verrall's ESP received the information and then projected a telepathic hallucination. However, the apparition represented someone who had been dead for ten years. The apparition may have been a hallucination engendered by telepathy, but if this were so the telepathy would have had to come from the dead woman.

A similar case which implies that apparitions of the dead are exactly what they appear to be is the apparition of J. L. Chaffin. Many apparitions have revealed information not known to the percipient until later verification is obtained. In the Chaffin case this information had such importance that it became the principal testimony in a legal case.

James L. Chaffin died in 1921. Upon his death the terms of his will were executed and his third son, Marshall, inherited his farm, thus leaving his wife and other three sons disinherited. The will was originally written and witnessed in November 1905.

In 1925, four years after his father's death, James P. Chaffin began having vivid "dreams" in which his father appeared to him. Finally after several such visions Chaffin reported that he saw his father's form next to his bed dressed as he had been in life and wearing an old black overcoat. The apparition finally spoke to his son: "You will find my will in my overcoat pocket." Chaffin was puzzled by this experience, yet so convinced of its reality that he contacted his mother and asked for the old coat. The coat, it seems, had been given to his brother John. Chaffin made the long journey to his brother's residence and found the coat. The lining of the pocket had been sewn up and inside was a piece of paper upon which was written, "Read the 27th chapter of Genesis in my daddie's old Bible."

Chaffin returned to his mother's house with his daughter and two other witnesses, Thomas Blackwelder and his daughter. The group had to search for the Bible but finally found it, after much travail, in a drawer. The Bible was so dilapidated that it fell apart when handled. Blackwelder picked up the part containing the Book of Genesis and on opening it found that two pages had been folded together into a pocket. Inside they found a handwritten, though perfectly legal will that Chaffin Sr. had written in 1919 which stated simply and concisely: "I, James L. Chaffin, do make my last will and testament and here it is. I want, after giving my body a decent burial, my little property equally divided between my four children, if they are living at my death, both personal and real estate divided equal and if not living, give share to their children. And if she is living, you must take care of your mammy. Now this is my last will and testament. Witness my hand and seal———(signed) James L. Chaffin, This January 16, 1919."

This second will was taken to court. During that time Chaffin Sr.'s phantom reappeared and again asked about his will. It was his last appearance. The second will was upheld as superseding the first since several witnesses could certify that the handwriting was authentic. The will was not contested as was planned and the estate was redistributed.

To be sure one can argue that theoretically the Chaffin will case does not necessarily prove that Chaffin survived death. Perhaps young Chaffin had become aware of the existence of the will via ESP. He unconsciously exteriorized a hallucination of his father (since Chaffin reported during the investigation that he was not really asleep when the phantom spoke, thus it was not a dream) to make this information known to the conscious mind. Perhaps it was also a case of cryptamnesia—a technical term meaning forgotten memory. That is, during his life the elder man had mentioned the will to his son, who had forgotten about it until, through his odd experience, the knowledge came to his conscious recollection.

These explanations are theoretically possible but they just do not fit the facts. First of all, Chaffin and all other family members adamantly stated that Chaffin Sr. had never mentioned a second will. In any event, those few cases of cryptamnesia on record usually occur during dreams, as in such cases where one dreams where one can find a lost object, the whereabouts of which was probably known to the unconscious all along. However, Chaffin's vision was not a dream, or at least he was reticent about calling it such. Also, if this were cryptamnesia, why did Chaffin continually see the phantom, even after finding the will? And finally, cryptamnesia would probably have led him to the Bible, not the script in the overcoat pocket.

These same arguments can be used against the ESP explanation. If, via ESP, Chaffin had either learned of the will through telepathy from his father while alive or clairvoyance after his death, why did the psi faculty lead him to the overcoat and not to the will itself? Again, why did the apparition have to appear so many times to relay the information? If the apparition was only a projection from Chaffin Jr. himself it certainly would have known when the will was found, yet it appeared again still inquiring about the will. The ESP theory just does not explain the case.

There is another possibility that I have always toyed with. Perhaps the case was a hoax. Young Chaffin forged the will, hid it in the Bible, made up the story about the apparition and then secreted the script in the old overcoat when he visited his brother. At first this explanation seems possible but it, too, can be disqualified. First of all, the will itself was old, yellowed, and obviously authentic. But more important is the fact that Chaffin would have known full well that the new will would be contested and would have to appear in the courts for probate—as in fact it did. (Marshall's widow and son backed out at the last minute when they realized they could not win the case.) Is it reasonable for a man attempting to win his case to present a story, which would have to be scrutinized thoroughly, that a ghost told him where to find the will? Certainly not. Chaffin could have just as well "accidentally found" the will at his mother's rather than risk the ridicule of the court and friends about "a spirit." The whole story was unnecessary to Chaffin's goal had the story been a hoax. In fact, such a "ghost story" would probably have severely jeopardized his claim rather than supported it.

However, if Chaffin's father's post-mortem personality did instigate the phantom all is explained. Obviously his father may have died worried about the injustice done to the others of his family and sought to rectify it. After many attempts he was able to contact his son through a telepathically created phantom or a form built up through some mysterious law of psychical phenomena. His earthly memory clouded, he confused the will with the note in his overcoat pocket. The phantom may not have been aware that the will had been found, which would explain his final appearance.

The counterexplanations are ingenious, but ingenuity does not constitute plausibility. In the Chaffin case no nonsurvivalistic theory can explain all the facts in the case. If we accept that the Chaffin phantom really was instigated by the personality of the dead father all inconsistencies of the case are cleared up.

Can one deny that some apparitions indicate that we survive death? In several instances apparitions have appeared which seem linked to a specific "death pact"—that whoever should die first would appear to the survivor. Such cases are common and are fairly stereotyped. For example, one person dies and soon appears to his death-pact friend as a crisis apparition. Later, the percipient learns of his friend's death at the exact moment. Many crisis apparitions have been included in this book and in themselves are only suggestive of survival, since they can, theoretically, be explained as telepathic hallucinations. But in some instances these apparitions appear so long after death, in answer to the death pact, that we are forced to assume that either (a) the phantom represents the deceased's surviving personality and motivation or (b) for absolutely no reason whatsoever, and while in perfect physical and mental health, the percipient suddenly has a vivid hallucination. Now, if one does not wish to believe in psychical phenomena there is no problem, for he can immediately assume that the apparitions are hallucinations projected by the viewers. But if one does believe in the phenomenon of apparitional experiences these death-pact cases, fulfilled only after several years, are hard to explain unless they are instigated by the dead, as seems to be the case of Miss E. M. T. who wrote: "I awoke from sleep and saw my brother who had been dead more than five years standing at the foot of my bed. He stood still, gazing at me earnestly. I cannot remember a voice but he distinctly conveyed to my mind the impression that I was to have no more anxiety, and that all would be for the best. I said, 'Oh, Arthur!' and jumped up to go to him, when he vanished. . . . My brother in life had said he would appear after death if possible."

Sometimes phantoms of the dead convey information not known to the percipient, as in the case of Lieutenant Sutton. If only ESP were involved why the necessity of a phantom at all? Why could not the percipient just have an ESP impression?

As I have repeatedly stressed, there is no general agreement on the survival issue in parapsychology. However, many researchers do feel that if all the evidence were taken and weighed, many psychical phenomena do indicate that man not only survives death but can affect the living as well. I share this view.

In any book such as this the author is expected to sum up his views and opinions about the topics he has presented—perhaps offering his own theories or at least his support for one theory to explain his data. I am afraid that I have no authoritative answer to what apparitions are, what laws govern their appearance, or what principles rule their mechanics. The reader may be a bit confused since sometimes I have favored the theory that apparitions are telepathic hallucinations, at other times that they are the "doubles" we all harbor within, and at still other moments a curious mixture of ESP and PK. The reason for this is that I doubt if there is really only one type of apparition. Apparitions may have many etiologies and I do not think that the existence of telepathic hallucinations outlaws the existence of totally objective phantoms. However, I do feel a bit uneasy when some parapsychologists argue in favor of one theory over another conveniently forgetting about cases that do not fit the theory they present.

As an investigator I have been fortunate to have experienced the psychical by personal experience, verifying the experiences of others, and by encountering the unseen during my research. I take for granted that psychical influences are part of our day-to-day lives. I see nothing occult about them but see them as natural, though rare, psychological phenomena that we will eventually understand. This attitude is hard-won since I had to wade through much nonsense in my search for the psychic. I have investigated ghosts that have turned out to be malfunctioning gas heaters; poltergeists that were children tricking their parents; apparitions that turned out to be reflections; psychics who were hysterics, liars, and psychotics. Yet in spite of all this disappointment came the experience of testing two good ESP subjects, one a housewife in Los Angeles and the other a blind girl being researched at UCLA; I have experienced a haunted house; I have worked with a gifted psychic; and finally I have had my own personal experiences.

I also take for granted that the dead might influence us. I began my career in parapsychology as an anti-survivalist. I was so confused by the quagmire of theories all of which *could* explain psychic phenomena that I could not see how the survival problem could ever be resolved. I began to question my cultural background and felt that belief in survival after death was an illusion. But after more study I started to realize that much psychic phenomena could be explained only if man survived death. The out-of-the-body experience was the first stepping stone. Then came the fact that communications through mediums could not *all* be explained by ESP. Deathbed visions also became unaccountable. Finally, I structured all my views into a book, *The Welcoming Silence,* to explain the cogency of the survival theory and why I support it.

I also believe that we survive death because of my own experiences as an investigator of the psychical. I am afraid that most parapsychologists have devoted so much time to experimental ESP that they have missed the opportunity to witness full-fledged spontaneous phenomena. It is no wonder many of them are nonsurvivalists—they have had so little contact with psychical manifestations.

I have been lucky enough to live in a haunted house and no

amount of theoretical dissertation could ever shake me from the conviction that what I have experienced in this house has shown willful motivation and intelligence. I have spoken to great mediums such as Ena Twigg and I cannot believe that their experiences were attributable to anything other than the dead. I cannot believe that the mind has tricked these psychics into believing that they saw and communicated with the dead when in fact it was solely their own ESP in masquerade. With a group of friends and colleagues I sat week after week in experimental séances trying to get the psychic to manifest. This was finally successful. So, after many encounters with the psychic my own firsthand experience leads me to accept that the dead can manifest to the living. A logical examination of the history and literature of the field has also supported this belief. Of course my own out-of-the-body experiences vividly brought home the fact that we are not only a material being, but a spiritual one as well.

Apparitions, as no other phenomenon, bring to the fore that man is a spiritual being. Although they serve as evidence for survival of death they also show that some faculty inherent in man has the ability to exceed both time and space. Far from being governed by our physical universe they transcend it. It is no wonder that so many who have experienced phantoms, whether by seeing an apparition or by having an out-of-the-body experience, acquire from that experience the belief that man is a far greater mystery than is the material universe in which we live. These people see in man a more complex entity than merely a mass of biological organs, cells, and atoms.

Apparitions have been recorded for centuries. They will be recorded for centuries more. They represent one of many unusual phenomena that penetrate our world along with ESP, mysterious Fortean phenomena of nature, and new dimensions of time and space. We live, quite literally, in a whole world of phantoms.

notes and references

(Note: If a source is given in the text the source is not cited in the references.)

1. A Variety of Phantoms

G. N. M. Tyrrell's classic study of apparitions was published as *Apparitions* (London, Gerald Duckworth, 1953). For van Dam experiments see the *Compte Rendu du Premier Congrès International des Recherches Psychiques à Copenhague,* 1921. William James wrote up his friend's experience in the *Journal:* ASPR, Vol. III, pp. 253–4. Beard's experiences are in *Phantasms of the Living* (London, Kegan Paul, 1886), and Mrs. Hurth's case was used by Ian Stevenson in his "Telepathic Impressions—A Review and Report of Thirty Five New Cases," *Proc:* ASPR, Vol. 29, pp. 61–198. The Bowyer-Bower case was used by Salter in his *Ghosts and Apparitions* (London, G. Bell, 1938), and the Paquet and Booth cases were published in the *Journal:* SPR, Vol. VII and Vol. VIII respectively. F. G.'s encounter is summarized in Myers's *The Human Personality and Its Survival of Bodily Death* (London, Longmans, 1903). Mr. MacKenzie's book is entitled *Apparitions and Ghosts* (London, Arthur Barker, 1971). For the Palladia case see *Proc:* SPR, Vol. X, pt. XXVI. Geley's work on Ossowiecki is in his *Clairvoyance and Materialization* (New York, Doran, 1924). Rose Morton's "Diary of a Haunted House" was published in the *Proc:* SPR, Vol. VIII, and Jung's comments and experiences are published in his collected works (Princeton University Press, 1961). The Savage case is in Minot J. Savage's *Can Telepathy Explain?* (New York, G. P. Putnam, 1903).

2. The Return from Silence

The major source for the Sutton case is George Thacher's report, "The Case of Lieut. James B. Sutton" *Journal:* ASPR, Vol. V. G. W. Lambert's opinion was expressed in the *Journal:* SPR, Vol. 46, pp. 212–3. The MacKenzie case can be found in the *Proc:* SPR, Vol. III, p. 95.

3. *Brushes with the Unseen*

The Bayless quote is from his *The Enigma of the Poltergeist* (West Nyack, N.Y., Parker Publishing Co., 1967). The Carrington case was used in his *The Invisible World* (New York, Beechhurst Press, 1946) and his odd "encounter" can be found in his *Psychic Oddities* (London, Rider & Co., 1952). The Bayless brothers' encounter is in Raymond Bayless' *Experiences of a Psychical Researcher* (New Hyde Park, N.Y., University Books, 1972). Guirdham's two experiences may be found respectively in his *Obsession* (London, Neville Spearman, 1972) and *The Cathars and Reincarnation* (London, Neville Spearman, 1970). Morris outlines animal reactions to the haunted house in *Theta,* #33, #34 [1971–2]. An-psi research is summarized by John Randall in the *Journal:* SPR, Vol. 46 (1972), pp. 124–34, and Stanford's experiment can be found in the *Journal:* ASPR, Vol. 64 (1970), pp. 161–86.

4. *Phantom Faces*

Goodrich-Freer's experience can be found in her book, *Essays in Psychical Research* (London, George Redway, 1899). For the *Watertown* case see Carrington's *The Invisible World* (New York, Beechhurst Press, 1946) and an article by Michael Mann, "The Watertown's Pursuing Ghosts," *Fate,* Dec. 1963. Cook's experiments may be found in *Journal:* ASPR, Vol. 10 (1916). The Belméz haunting particulars were given me directly by Professor Hans Bender.

5. *Phantom Voices*

For the Willington Mill case see the *Journal:* SPR, Vol. V. The Huguenot case was published in Thurston's *Ghosts and Poltergeists* (Chicago, Gateway Edition, 1954). The Blake material was published by David Abbott in his "History of a Strange Case," *Proc:* ASPR for 1913 and later as a booklet. Roll's experiments with Jurgenson appeared as a report circulated by the Psychical Research Foundation. Raudive's work can be read in his book, *Breakthrough* (New York, Taplinger Publishing Co., 1971). The von Szalay experiments are in a letter in the ASPR *Journal,* Jan. 1959. The author's experiments are in the *Journal of Paraphysics,* Vol. 4.

6. *Fiery Phantoms*

Kate Christie's book *Apparitions* was published by Routledge and Kegan Paul, 1965. For the Burton case see Crookall's *More Astral Projections,* (London, Aquarian Press, 1964). For the Du Cane case refer to *Journal:* SPR, Vol. V; the Davis case is printed in the *Proc:* SPR, Vol VI. Osis's research is outlined in the Newsletter of the ASPR #14. Larsen's case can be found in Crookall's *More Astral*

Projections. For Zingaropoli's study see the *Annals of Psychical Science*, Sept. 1909. The Denza case can be found in the same publication, Dec. 1908 issue. Joüet's researches were published in various issues of *Le Purgatoire*, circa 1900.

7. Wild Hauntings!

For the Calvados haunting see Flammarion's *Haunted Houses* (New York, Appleton, 1924). All of the Roll cases are summarized in his book *The Poltergeist* (New York, New American Library, 1973). Barrett's cases were reported by him in the *Proc:* SPR, Vol. 25. Lombroso's case can be found in his *After Death—What?* (Boston, Small, Maynard & Co., 1909), Stevenson's views were presented in the *Journal:* ASPR, Vol. 66 (1972). The Landau case appears in the *Journal:* SPR, Vol. 42. For the Arthur Osborn case see his book, *The Superphysical* (London, Ivor Nicholson and Watson, 1937). For the Brook House haunting see the *Review of Reviews* for 1892.

8. Haunted Houses Today

The Bremen affair was reported in the *Proc:* of the Parapsychological Association, No. 5. The history of Abbey House is in the *Journal:* SPR, Vol. 46. Bayless describes his encounter with a haunted house in his *Enigma of the Poltergeist*. Mrs. Baterbaugh's experiences were included in a paper by Murphy and Klemme in the *Journal:* ASPR, Vol. 60. The three cases investigated by the Psychical Research Foundation are in *Theta*, #20, #23 and #27 respectively. Schmeidler's investigation is found in the *Journal:* ASPR, Vol. 60, and Watkins reported his experiments at the 15th Annual Convention of the Parapsychological Association and to the author personally.

9. Further Phantoms

Hyslop's study of deathbed visions was published in an article in the *Journal:* ASPR, Jan. 1907, and also in his book, *Psychical Research and the Resurrection* (Boston, Small, Maynard & Co., 1908). The Ogle case can be found in the *Proc:* SPR, Vol. 5. Barrett's cases, including Warcollier's report, are in his book, *Deathbed Visions* (London, Methuen, 1926). The Demler case is in the *Bulletin:* Boston Society for Psychic Research, Sept. 1931. Smokey's appearance is reported in *Phantasms of the Living*, and Helen Daniels wrote up her experiences in the *Journal:* ASPR, Vol. XXXV. The Kluski material can be found in Geley's *Clairvoyance and Materialization*, and Pawlowski's article "The Mediumship of Franek Kluski of Warsaw," *Journal:* ASPR, Vol. XIX. Venzano's case was reported in the *Annals of Psychical Science* for Aug.–Sept. 1907.

10. The Phantom Within

For Hart's thesis see his "Six Theories about Apparitions," *Proc.;* SPR, Vol. 50. The Bertrand case can be found in the *Proc:* SPR, Vol. VIII, p. 194. All the

Crookall material can be found in his books: *Case-book of Astral Projection* (New Hyde Park, N.Y., University Books, 1972), *The Study and Practice of Astral Projection* (London, Aquarian Press, 1961), *Mor Astral Projections* (London, Aquarian Press, 1964), *Intimations of Immortality* (London, James Clarke, 1965), and *Out-of-the-Body Experiences: A fourth analysis* (New Hyde Park, N.Y., University Books, 1970).

11. Toward a New Reality

For the Paterson case see Salter's *Ghosts and Apparitions*. For the surveys of spontaneous cases see articles by J. B. Rhine, *Journal of Parapsychology*, Vol. 17; G. Sannwald, *Zeitschrift für Parapsychologie und Grenzgebeite der Psychologie*, Vol. 3; J. Prasad and I. Stevenson, *Inter. Journal of Parapsychology*, Vol. X; C. Green, *Journal:* SPR, Vol. 53. The cases of George Johnston, Mrs. F., and the dream-ESP cases are all cited in the Salter volume. Dunne's dream records are in his book, *An Experiment with Time* (London, Faber & Faber, 1927). The Maimonides dream research is summarized in Ullman-Krippner-Vaughan's *Dream Telepathy* (New York, Macmillan, 1973). For the Janet-Richet case see Richet's *30 Years of Psychical Research* (New York, Macmillan, 1923). The Krippner-Honorton study is in the *Journal:* ASPR, Vol. 63. The Morales case is reported in J. L. Wilkins's *Devil Trees and Plants of Africa, Asia and South America* (Girard, Kansas, Haldeman-Julius, 1948), and the Masters-Houston research and reports are in their *The Varieties of Psychedelic Experience* (New York, Holt, Rinehart & Winston, 1965). The two cases of unrecognized phantoms are taken from the *Proc:* SPR, Vol X, pt. XXVI. The Bermuda Triangle is summarized in Vincent Gaddis' *Invisible Horizons* (New York, Chilton, 1965). Other Fortean phenomena are fully discussed in Fort's *The Book of the Damned* (Boni & Liveright, 1919) and Gould's *Oddities* (London, Geoffrey Bles, 1928). Mrs. Verrall's case is reported in *Proc:* SPR, Vol X, pt. XXVI. The Chaffin will case is in the *Journal:* SPR, Nov. 1927. Mrs. E. M. T.'s case was drawn from the *Proc:* SPR, Vol. X, pt. XXVI.

suggested reading

Barrett, William. *Deathbed Visions* (London, Methuen & Co., 1926).

Apparitions have long served as prime evidence for life after death. Barrett collected several accounts of apparitions seen by the dying and the reports of those at deathbeds who had similar experiences. The most important feature is that often those dying report visions of apparitions representing persons they had no normal way of knowing had died. The volume is a classic.

Bayless, Raymond. *Animal Ghosts* (New Hyde Park, N.Y., University Books, 1970).

Animal apparitions have often been reported. This is one of the few books that covers this fascinating topic as well as integrating it with the whole realm of animal ESP and survival after death.

Bayless, Raymond. *Apparitions and Survival of Death* (New Hyde Park, N.Y., University Books, 1973).

Probably the most complete and scholarly book in print on apparitions of all types. As the title implies, the data is especially geared toward the question of whether or not apparitions serve as an indicator of survival after death. The author believes so. The book also includes much material on the out-of-the-body experience.

Bayless, Raymond. *The Enigma of the Poltergeist* (West Nyack, N.Y., Parker Publishing Co., 1967).

There are two types of book that can be written about poltergeists: a general summary of famous cases or personal investigations. This volume is not only a general survey of cases and what we know about the poltergeist, but an analysis of several of the author's personal investigations. Also available in paperback.

Carrington, Hereward, and Fodor, Nandor. *Haunted People* (New York, E. P. Dutton, 1951).

This handy release, also available in paperback, contains a chronology and descriptions of all recorded poltergeist cases from antiquity to the present. More detailed analyses are made of selected cases. Fodor's section of the book contains psychoanalytical evaluations of several poltergeist cases. This material is highly speculative.

Collins, B. Abdy. *The Cheltenham Ghost* (London, Psychic Press, 1948).

A complete analysis of the "Morton Ghost." Also included are general discussions of apparitions, hauntings, and theories to account for them.

Flammarion, Camille. *Haunted Houses* (New York, D. Appleton & Co., 1924).

A masterly review of several European hauntings including a complete résumé of the wild events at Calvados Castle. Flammarion also grapples with the explanation for hauntings and favors the theory that post-mortem intelligences are involved. A very complete book on "haunted houses" and one of the best books available on the subject.

Fodor, Nandor. *On the Trail of the Poltergeist* (New York, Citadel Press, 1958).

A fascinating story of a hunt for a poltergeist in England. Although Fodor could never make up his mind whether there was anything genuine in the case, his main interest was the psychological factors behind it. No matter what Fodor thought, the case has all the earmarks of being genuine. Fodor was a better psychoanalyst than investigator.

Goodrich-Freer, A., and John, Marquess of Bute (editors). *The Alleged Haunting of B—— House* (London, George Redway, 1899).

A day-by-day diary of a haunted house by the psychical researchers who rented it for investigation. Also included are the testimonies of several other individuals who were invited to spend a night in the house. Makes Shirley Jackson's novel *The Haunting of Hill House* look like small beer in comparison.

Jaffé, Aniela. *Apparitions and Precognition* (New Hyde Park, N.Y., University Books, 1962).

A European collection of modern apparition cases. There is little evidence for the cases which are mostly just personal anecdotes but they are fascinating nonetheless. Dr. Jaffé is a Jungian psychologist so one must wade through a lot of Jungian interpretations of the cases. Just as with the cases themselves, there is little evidence for the interpretations.

MacKenzie, Andrew. *Apparitions and Ghosts* (London, Arthur Barker, 1971).

Another modern collection of apparition cases which the author has tried to substantiate as well as compare to older cases collected by the SPR. Special consideration is given the "Morton Ghost." One of the few recent books on apparitions that is scholarly as well as interesting and geared to the nonspecialist reader.

MacKenzie, Andrew. *A Gallery of Ghosts* (New York, Taplinger, 1973).

In his second book on apparitions MacKenzie has tried to evaluate encounters with phantoms as recorded by famous writers in their works, and compare them to more evidential cases published by the SPR. Also included are reports of apparitions and similar phenomena by researchers such as Cesare Lombroso, A. R. G. Owen, and Frank Podmore.

Osis, Karlis. *Deathbed Observations by Physicians and Nurses* (New York, Parapsychology Foundation, 1961).

Taking a lead from Barrett, Dr. Osis sent out thousands of questionnaires to doctors and nurses to see if Barrett's data about visions of the dying could be substantiated. Osis confirmed that the dying have inexplicable apparitional experiences not due to any organic factor caused by their illness or medication.

Owen, A. R. G. *Can We Explain the Poltergeist?* (New York, Garrett Publications, 1954).

The classic on poltergeists. Owen gives a fairly complete catalogue of historical cases mixed in with a discussion of the various types of poltergeistic phenomena. Included is a case Owen was concerned in plus much material on psychological and physical factors involved in the phenomenon of the poltergeist.

Price, Harry. *Poltergeist over England* (London, Country Life Ltd., 1945).

A popularly written history of English poltergeist cases. Price does not make a clear differentiation between hauntings and poltergeists and both are represented in this lengthy volume.

Roll, W. G. *The Poltergeist* (Garden City, N.Y., Doubleday, 1972).

This is an analysis of several poltergeist cases investigated by the author. In several of them Mr. Roll was able to witness the phenomena in action. Although not a comprehensive book, other cases are cited and the author gives an in-depth consideration to the psychological and physical factors involved.

Salter, W. H. *Ghosts and Apparitions* (London, G. Bell & Sons, 1938).

A short anthology and discussion of apparition cases collected and analyzed by the SPR. Also included is a chapter on hauntings and one on poltergeists which Salter dismisses as having little evidential value.

Thurston, Herbert. *Ghosts and Poltergeists* (Chicago, Henry Regnery, 1954).

Thurston was a Catholic priest and a critical hard-core investigator of psychical phenomena. The book is a compilation of his writings on several poltergeist cases.

Tyrrell, G. N. M. *Apparitions* (London, Duckworth & Co., 1953).

For many this is the authoritative text on apparitions. The different types are outlined and Tyrrell examines the various theories promulgated to explain them. Finally his own difficult-to-comprehend theory that apparitions are nonphysical is offered. Hornell Hart pointed out the problems inherent in Tyrrell's theory and superseded it with his "Six Theories about Apparitions," *Proc:* SPR, Vol. 50.

index